Reformed Christians and Mormon Christians:

Let's Talk!

Reformed Christians and Mormon Christians: Let's Talk!

by

Roger R. Keller

Pryor Pettengill
1986

Library of Congress Catalog Card Number: 86-63129
ISBN 0-933462-06-9

To Flo Beth
with
Love and Thanks

Contents

Preface

Since the time this book was begun, pressures against Mormons have continued to mount all across the country. Some people seem convinced that Christ has called them to destroy, in his name, a group of persons professing the Christian faith, since their doctrines differ from those of their antagonists. How sad it is when people feel compelled on religious grounds to pit themselves against other people. In this author's eyes, the very desire to destroy another person's beliefs, in the name of some higher religious principle, is the denial of that principle. Thus, the only path to a healthy Christian community is the path of understanding and compassion—not the convoluted trail of religious arrogance or intellectual superiority.

Each of us comes to any human relationship with a set of "preconceived notions." If we seek ugliness in people, we will find it. But it is also true, that if we seek the good in others, we will find that, too. I have sought to *understand* my Mormon brothers and sisters as I have written these pages. I have tried to let doctrines stand side by side, allowing the reader thoughtfully and prayerfully to draw his or her own conclusions. In the end, I believe that God is greater than all of us combined, and that he uses many paths to lead us to himself in Jesus Christ. We all stand under his Lordship, regardless of denominational or religious affiliations. Perhaps we should learn that he can make *all* human attempts to understand him and to worship him in Jesus Christ beautiful. Only people make the search for God a thing of darkness and dishonor.

Agreement on the content of this book is not sought from either the Reformed community or the Mormon community. Each reader would have stated things differently. However, what is sought is (1) the honest wrestling of every reader with his or her own personal relationship to the God who has made himself known in Jesus Christ; and (2) the openness to love and appreciate a religiously diverse neighbor. If through prayer, Bible study, and discussion, the faith and love of Christians of all denominations are deepened, I can seek no greater personal reward.

I extend my deepest thanks and appreciation to my Mormon friends, Darl Andersen and David K. Udall, for their support and observations as the manuscript of this book was prepared. Dr. Truman G. Madsen, holder of the Chair of Christian Understanding at Brigham Young University, deserves special thanks for his willingness to read and re-read the manuscript, offering comments for consideration and resources to be consulted. My long-time friend, the Rev. Dr. Paul J. Baird, has also rendered immensely valuable insights as he read these pages through the eyes of a Reformed theologian who grew up in "Mormon country." Finally, my thanks to Mr. Gary P. Gillum, Ancient Studies Bibliographer in the Brigham Young University library, who provided invaluable assistance in background research, and to Mrs. Doris Brower, without whose help the typing of the manuscript would have been long delayed.

April 1985
Roger R. Keller

Abbreviations

D & C	Doctrine and Covenants. One of the standard Mormon works containing revelations to the prophets of The Church of Jesus Christ of Latter-day Saints
Doctrines	Joseph Fielding Smith, *Doctrines of Salvation*, 3 volumes.
HC	Joseph Smith, *History of the Church*, 6 volumes.
JS-H	*Joseph Smith: History*. Found in the *Pearl of Great Price* (another of the Mormon standard works) along with the Books of Moses and Abraham.
KJV	King James Translation of the Bible.
RSV	Revised Standard Version (Translation) of the Bible.
Teachings	Joseph Smith, *Teachings of the Prophet Joseph Smith*.

Citations from the Old and New Testaments and the Book of Mormon use abbreviations standard to each work.

Introduction

Setting the Stage

Peacemaking is Christ's call to all persons in all walks of life, in every social situation, and within any national boundary. For Christians of the Presbyterian tradition, peacemaking is a stated goal of the General Assembly, and thus of the total Presbyterian Church. Too often, we think of peacemaking as something that is global in nature, as something that deals only with nuclear weaponry, and, thus, as something that we in our own small ways can never affect or bring about. The reality is, of course, that the opportunities for peacemaking are myriad, and that they are very close at hand for all of us. True, we have limited ability to influence the international issues of peace, but we have a great deal of ability to influence within our own communities the peace, or lack thereof, that exists between social groups, between cultural entities, between persons of different racial groupings, and between persons of different religious backgrounds. The fundamental purpose of this book is to help bridge one gap that exists within Christendom—i.e., the gap between Christians who are called Mormons and Christians of the Reformed tradition. Mormons are those who are members of The Church of Jesus Christ of Latter-day Saints. "Reformed" means those denominations which have followed the teachings of Calvin (e.g., Presbyterians, Dutch Reformed).

Human beings have a tendency to believe that they can capture in words and define in structures the nature of God and the way God should behave. Each of us tends to believe that we know more about God than does our neighbor and that our knowledge is accurate and indisputable. If we really stop to think about these assumptions, we can only define them as notions that manifest a great deal of human arrogance. In actuality, we cannot hold, with any true theological integrity, that God's grace and power are limited to the human boundaries in which we would choose to capture them. God is not arrogant, elitist, or prejudiced. Only human beings bear those traits, and when we carry those characteristics over into our religious lives and our relationships with our religiously diverse neighbors, sparks fly, barriers go up, and animosity reigns. Almost without exception, the sparks, the animosities, and the barriers, are generated by a failure to understand and to appreciate the positions of those who differ from us. It is particularly sad to see deep divisions between persons who claim the Christian faith, for Christ's body was never meant to be fractured and fragmented. Each division or denomination that we as human beings create is a blot on Christ's Universal Church. Because of human sin and human frailties, the Church will likely never become a single entity, but it need not be a complex of disparate and divergent traditions which will not even communicate with one another. Rather, under the common lordship of Jesus Christ, the Church with all its diversity should be able to celebrate its unity, as its members come to understand more completely the beauty and the depth of the faith of those who see Christ and his work in slightly different colors. In particular, the animosities that have existed over the past 150 years between Christians of the "main-line denominations" and Christians of the Mormon tradition are both inexcusable and unnecessary. We are all Christians who confess Jesus Christ as Lord and Savior. We are all Christians who confess that God has made himself known in Jesus Christ.

Mesa, Arizona, is a community that was founded by Mormon settlers in the latter part of the 19th century. Thus, its traditions and its people have been predominantly Mormon. But now, the community is changing, and many more persons of other religious traditions are moving to Mesa. Today, the Mormon people are not numerically in the majority, and yet their history and their traditions still deeply influence the life and decisions of the community. When I arrived in Mesa, I discovered two basic things: (1) the knowledge of Christians who were not Mormons about their Mormon neighbors was very poor and terribly inaccurate; but (2) those same non-Mormon persons were deeply interested in what their Mormon neighbors actually did believe. When my congregation learned that I had been a member of The Church of Jesus Christ of Latter-day Saints for a short period of time, they requested that I teach a class about the faith of the Mormons. After some basic discussions about our own Reformed traditions, I complied with that request, and taught a six-week class on the Mormon faith, utilizing members of the Mormon community to convey as accurately as possible the actual beliefs of the Mormon church. It was a tremendously successful class, and out of it came a new appreciation of the Mormon faith among the Presbyterian people who attended. As the Mormon people discovered that their faith was not being denigrated or unfairly presented, they developed a desire to learn more about Presbyterians and other denominations within the Christian tradition. Thus, an invitation was issued by the Maricopa Stake for Presbyterians to speak to them about what it means to be a Presbyterian. This contact led to invitations to the Catholics and the Methodists to present similar programs. As a result, the religious tenor and interrelationships within the community of Mesa have improved. This change is perhaps epitomized by the community Thanksgiving services in which Jews, Catholics, Mormons, Presbyterians, Methodists, Episcopalians, and members of the Christian Church all worship together before their common God. Further, the Mesa Ecumenical Clergy Association issued an invitation to the Mormon church to appoint a representative to sit with the Association as they discussed ways to address the problems of the community from the standpoint of religious commitment. Through this book, it is hoped that the message can be conveyed to persons in other communities like Mesa that differences in theology should not separate Christian from Christian when, in fact, unity lies in the common confession that Jesus is Lord.

Purpose of This Book

The first purpose of any book dealing with faith should be to deepen the faith of all who read it. That can happen as people come to understand the traditions of others more completely, and as they then reflect on their own traditional beliefs. Thus, this book is written for all persons of faith, but primarily for lay-Christians of the Reformed tradition and Christians of the Mormon tradition, so that they may learn to appreciate and to respect the faith of one another.

It is also hoped that this book can serve a useful purpose among ministers of the Reformed tradition or other traditions who find themselves serving in "Mormon country." In my experience, ministers have often served as a dividing force within communities of faith, because some of them appear to believe that it is "proper theology," rather than a proper relationship with one's Lord, that makes a person Christian. Thus, as ministers of various traditions wrestle with the content of this book, it is hoped that they will come to a broader appreciation of their Mormon neighbors and the depth of the Mormon faith. At the same time, it is hoped that Mormon Bishops, Stake Presidents, and missionaries will gain an appreciation of the depth of faith and commitment to Jesus Christ held by persons not of their own tradition. Because Mormon faith principally looks back to 1830 or prior to 100 A.D., there is a great deal of Church thought and Church faith that is not part of the Mormon heritage, nor is it part of their knowledge. In that sense Mormons have missed a great deal of the depth and beauty of mainline Christian thought. As Mormons read the pages of this book, perhaps they, too, will gain a deeper appreciation for the commitment of their religiously diverse neighbors.

Finally, as persons assimilate the following material, it is hoped that they will also struggle with their personal faith, ask questions about it, and find themselves strengthened in their commitments to their Lord. People should learn that Christ through the Holy Spirit calls many individuals to serve him in many ways.

It is human arrogance to believe that Christ *must* limit his work only to one structure or to one tradition. Thus, Christ's Spirit pervades the missionary activity of us all, calling many to serve him by using various denominations as his tools to complete the act of universal reconciliation, which finds its focus in the incarnation, death, and resurrection of the one Lord Jesus Christ.

Format of the Book

This book will contain three basic parts. The first part will deal with our roots and individual identities as Reformed Christians and Mormon Christians. In it we will look briefly at the founders of our individual traditions. We will look at the roots of our perceived authority and at the organization that undergirds each tradition. Further, we will examine the missionary activities of our traditions and the rationale for approaching persons both inside and outside the Church. In addition, we will consider some of the excesses that missionary activities have generated and some of the hard feelings that have come from these activities.

In the second part of the book, we will ask about the fundamental, underlying theological principles of each tradition. We will explore the sources of our individual testimonies, the role and function of scripture as it relates to ecclesiastical traditions, and most importantly, we will examine the role and function of Jesus Christ in the Reformed tradition and in the Mormon tradition. Other topics will include the divine intentionality in creating human beings, God's history of salvation with his people, and the relationship between faith and works. We will conclude with a brief segment on the relationship between Christians and Jews as viewed by the two traditions. Part

Three will simply ask the question, "Where can we go from here?"

In each of the first two parts, every chapter will state both the Mormon position and the Reformed position on the issues at hand. There will be a final section to each chapter entitled "Reflections," which will seek to provide an opportunity for readers to consider the differences and similarities that exist between the Mormon and the Reformed traditions. Further, readers will be summoned to consider whether there may not be some ground in their own faith tradition which, at a minimum, can heighten their kinship, their love and their respect for neighbors of a sister faith.

Finally, my presentation of the Reformed faith will have a decidedly Barthian tone. I personally find in Karl Barth's *Church Dogmatics* the bringing together of all that is powerful and profound from our ancestors in the faith— both Catholic and Protestant. He is thorough; he is complete; and he writes for the Church—the community of faith. I pray that this book may be a contribution to the spiritual growth of persons within Christ's Universal Church.

Part One:
Who Are We?

"I Am the Vine,   1
You Are the Branches"
John 15:5

Joseph Smith: The Beginning of a New Branch

The Religious Climate of Upstate New York

To come to an understanding of Joseph Smith, we must seek a general understanding of the religious climate of western New York in the early 1800's, as well as seeking to determine how Joseph Smith was affected by it. To that end, we could turn to detailed histories of New York in the early 19th century, or we could turn to Joseph Smith's own narrative about his experiences in that period of time, or we could look at both. One of the difficulties with existing literature is that it tends to concentrate either on the details of secular history, or it concentrates on Joseph Smith's experience. Few try to bring the two accounts together. This is simply a must.

Joseph Smith writes (JS-H 1:1–5) that he was born December 23, 1805, in the town of Sharon, Vermont. When he was about ten his family moved to Palmyra, New York, and it was in this region that his story as a religious person really began. Smith notes that during his early teens there was a great deal of revivalistic activity taking place around his home. He reports that this generated great confusion in his mind, for the love and concern that should have been developed for one's neighbor as a product of religious commitment and conversion was not evident. His own family was caught up in the religious excitement of the day, and Smith's mother, Lucy, his brothers, Hyrum and

Samuel Harrison, and his sister, Sophronia, all joined the Presbyterian Church. Joseph himself was influenced to consider where he wanted to be aligned denominationally, and indicates that he was attracted to the Methodists. Yet, he was not sure of his relationship with any church, because of his confusion over the wrangling that took place between the various religious bodies (JS-H 1:7–8). He spells out that confusion graphically when he says:

> "For, not withstanding the great love which the converts to these different faiths expressed at the time of their conversion, the great zeal manifested by the respective clergy, who were active in getting up and promoting this extraordinary scene of religious feeling, in order to have everybody converted, as they were pleased to call it, let them join what sect they pleased; yet when the converts began to file off, some to one party and some to another, it was seen that the seemingly good feelings of both the priests and the converts were more pretended than real; for a scene of great confusion and bad feeling ensued—priest contending against priest, and convert against convert; so that all their good feelings one for another, if they ever had any, were entirely lost in the strife of words and a contest about opinions." (JS-H 1:6)

There seems to be no reason to doubt that, in the mind of a boy in his early and mid-teens, there was significant confusion about the religious ideas that his society considered to be important. Historical studies, and even studies radically opposed to the Mormon faith, generally agree that there was a significant amount of evangelism taking place between 1815 and 1820 in the region of Joseph Smith's home. The intensity of that activity is not particularly important. Rather, the decidedly important element is Joseph Smith's response to it. Clearly there was confusion, and Joseph sought to solve that confusion through the reading of scripture. He relates that one night, as he was reading in the Epistle to James, he read the following statement in chapter 1, verse 5 (KJV): "If any of you lack wisdom, let him ask of God, that giveth to all men liberally, and upbraideth not; and it shall be given to him" (JS-H 1:9–13). This passage had a tremendous impact on him. After a period of time, he finally decided to seek the wisdom of God through prayer, and it was this decision which ultimately led him to the grove, where he had his first visionary experience.

Joseph Smith's Visions (1820 to 1827)

Joseph says that his first vision occurred in the spring of 1820 (JS-H 1:14–20). He went out to a grove in the woods, where he knelt down and began to pray, seeking guidance concerning the various denominations. Smith relates that a dark presence seemed to overshadow and overwhelm him. Just as he was about to give himself up to the darkness, he saw a shaft of light descending from above him which drove the darkness away. In the light he saw two personages, one of whom pointed to the other saying, "This is my beloved son. Hear him!" Since Smith's object in praying was to determine which denomination to join, he was told that none of the existing denominations was correct, and that he should join no church. He then says that as he regained his normal senses following the vision, he found himself lying on his back in an extremely weakened condition. This concludes his account of the first vision.

Some persons, who have researched the first vision in detail, hold that there are varied accounts of that first vision. This is true. But the question must be raised whether variations in an account of a visionary experience may not well be expected. Modern studies in the functioning of memory have shown that human memory is at times highly selective. Further, differing times, perspectives, and audiences determine the content of a person's recollections. The fact that the accounts indicate that Joseph did not always state whether he encountered one or two persons is not surprising. But whatever the precise content of that first vision, it clearly had a tremendous impact upon Joseph Smith. (See Milton V. Backman, "Joseph Smith's Recitals of the First Vision," *The Ensign*, January 1985, pp. 8–17.)

Joseph apparently did not keep the vision to himself. He says that he communicated his experience to one of the Methodist preachers who had been active in the revival movements in his area, and that he was surprised at the negative response he received (JS-H 1:21–26). From the increasingly negative reactions that he recounts, it would seem that he was not initially shy about imparting his experience. Yet, he never denied the vision, nor could he, for it was part and parcel of his own religious experience.

For roughly three years after his first vision, Joseph Smith continued to pursue his daily life. The only new element was that he says he experienced persecution for his continued assertions that he had seen a vision. He admitted that he did not always behave as he believed he should have—i.e., as one having received a vision. He indicates that, "I frequently fell into many foolish errors, and displayed the weakness of youth, and the foibles of human nature" (JS-H 1:28). In a word, though he felt called of God, he did not always live in an exemplary way. Thus, he continued to live life on a day-by-day basis with his friends.

Finally, in 1823, Joseph seems to have come to the point of needing to know more of what God wished for him. Thus, one evening in September, he knelt by his bed and prayed for further guidance. He states that he experienced the gradual lightening of his room, and in the center of the light he found himself confronted with a personage who identified himself as a messenger of God named Moroni. He communicated to Joseph that God had a number of things which he would call Smith to accomplish. Moroni then instructed Smith about some metallic plates bearing the record of an ancient people who had inhabited this western continent in prior times. He also spoke of two stones which would be used to translate those plates. Additionally, he told of a priesthood, and quoted passages from both the Old and the New Testaments in support of it (Mal. 3 and 4, Is. 11, Acts 3:22–23, Joel 2:28 ff). That night Joseph experienced a vision of the plates and their location. Moroni then withdrew. This vision occurred twice more that same night, with virtually the same content each time. When the visionary experiences ended, Joseph realized it was morning. He went out to do his daily chores, but was weakened significantly by the experiences, and thus his father sent him home (JS-H 1:24–48).

On the way home, Joseph, as he was crossing a fence, fell to the ground and then experienced once again the appearance of Moroni. He was told to tell his father of his experiences, and his father's response was supportive. Joseph then went to the place where the plates were buried, which he had seen in his vision the night before. According to Smith, he went to a hill outside the city of Manchester, and there found a stone box with the plates in it. When he attempted to remove them, the angel would not permit him to do so. He was told to leave them there and to return to that spot once every year. Smith says that he followed the angel's instruction, and in each annual meeting received new understanding of what God would require of him (JS-H 1:49–54).

Finally, four years later on September 22, 1827, Joseph Smith was given permission to remove the plates from the ground and to take them with him for translation. Despite his best efforts to keep the plates secure, he relates that people kept trying to get them from him (JS-H 1:59–60). Many more visions occurred after this point in time, and some of these will be considered in later chapters. However, for an initial understanding, it is only necessary to review the first vision and the subsequent visions involving Moroni, all of which led to the point in time when Joseph Smith says that he began to translate the plates.

The Necessity of a Restoration

As has been seen, Joseph Smith appears to have been struggling with his personal religious response in the context of a very mixed and volatile religious situation in upstate New York. As one reads his writings, it becomes very clear that he was a man deeply steeped in scripture. He was a man of faith, and thus, a man seeking to respond to God's calling as he understood it. Unless one is willing simply to claim that Joseph Smith was an out-and-out fraud, one must agree that he was a man who experienced extraordinary spiritual events through his visionary experiences. This complex of religious fervor and religious experience led him to the conclusion that Christ's Church on earth had at best been polluted, and at worst, no longer existed in a recognizable form. Thus, he came to believe that Christ must restore his Church with all of its power and authority. Through his religious experiences Smith came to understand himself to be called to be the herald of a new dispensation, a new age, the latter-days which were to be ruled directly by Christ through his Restored Church. Joseph Smith understood this Church to be The Church of Jesus Christ of Latter-day Saints, as established through him and made visible through his followers. In his eyes, The Church of Jesus Christ of Latter-day Saints was not a new branch on an old vine, but rather it was the true vine itself. Other denominations through their quarreling and apparent lack of love and acceptance of one another had, in Joseph's view, ceased to bear Christ's full authority. Thus, he understood his work and his role to be that of prophet in the sense that he called people to obedience to the Lord's will and the Lord's ways in much the same way that the Old Testament prophets did. He was an agent, but never someone to be worshipped. His function and role were always subordinate to Jesus Christ, and it was always Jesus Christ that he sought to serve. This is not to say that he was not human with all the sins and foibles that go with that estate. His reflections and his diaries make his humanity and his quest for the grace of Christ obvious. The question that the non-Mormon Christian must eventually face is whether God might have used Joseph Smith, just as he has used other fragile and sinful people through time.

The Reformed Faith: An Historic Branch

In the Church's history the Reformed tradition is not perceived as discontinuous with that which preceded it. Those who identify with the Reformed tradition are deeply aware that their roots lie in the first century Church, and that they stand in continuity with that early Church. They have also participated in and grown out of the Roman Catholic tradition. Initially, the Reformation was not designed to be the birth of a new church. Luther sought only to deal with ills within Roman Catholicism which he felt were at variance with scripture and a violation of the basic ethical and moral stances which Christ calls all Christians to take. Through the avenues of academic debate and discussion, Luther believed that the Catholic Church could be cleansed of unhealthy practices and could continue to move ahead as the people of God. But Luther's concerns struck at the very heart of the organization and authority of Roman Catholicism. He questioned the role and function of the Pope and of the priesthood. He questioned whether there was only a select group of people, the priests, who were to mediate God's grace to the masses, or whether, in fact, all people had direct access to the knowledge of God's grace as it was made available to them within the pages of Holy Scripture. Sadly, both the Catholic Church and the followers of Luther became unalterably set in their positions, and the inevitable occurred. The body of Christ was torn asunder.

We in this age can look back and appreciate the many common points that existed between the Catholic Church and the Reformers. We find ourselves shaking our heads at the tragic divisions that have occurred between Catholics and Protestants. Presbyterians include in their *Book of Confessions* and in their worship services the Apostles' Creed and the Nicene Creed, both of which are utilized within the Catholic tradition. The basic boundaries of the Reformed and Catholic faiths are the same, and certainly Jesus Christ is central to both. Today, rather than arguing and defending territory, many members of both the Catholic and Reformed traditions are seeking ways to heal differences and to bridge misunderstandings, so that Christ's Church may at least move forward in harmony, if not in unity.

Mormons have traditionally neglected the history of the Church between 100 A.D. and 1830 A.D. Their typical

9

position has been that the Church lapsed into a period of ignorance in the Dark Ages and in the medieval period. But today Mormon and non-Mormon historians alike have demonstrated graphically that the role and function of the Church, in what was known as the Dark Ages, was in fact very vital to the maintenance, growth, and development of western society and culture. True, social structures were in constant flux, but at the same time there was tremendous activity in literature, the arts, music, and certainly in the life of the Church. Competent historians today have virtually dropped the term "Dark Ages" from their vocabulary, for they recognize that it is a misnomer. Therefore, contemporary Mormon scholarship does not argue that Christ's power and influence ever disappeared totally from the Church, even in the "Dark Ages." Instead, they would hold that while Christ never left the Church completely desolate, *in the light of the restoration* in 1830 it is now clear that certain essential elements had been lost from the Church which Christ had to reintroduce in the latter-days. Thus, Christ was actively involved in the Church through the centuries, actually calling the Reformers and laying the groundwork for the restoration. With the restoration came the return of the priesthood (and thus the Church's right to act with *authority* in Christ's name) and the opening once again of the celestial kingdom to all believers. The Mormons would agree with their Presbyterian brothers and sisters that the Church is always reforming, but would at the same time see the restoration as the culmination and fulfilment of all preceding reformations carried out under Christ's lordship.

There are three giants of the Reformation toward whom Presbyterians look as they consider the fathers of their tradition. These persons are Martin Luther (Germany), John Calvin (Switzerland), and John Knox (Scotland). Each in his own way established some of the fundamental principles of the Reformed tradition to which Presbyterians and others of this same tradition still adhere. The emphasis on God's approach to all humanity, the centrality of Jesus Christ, the priesthood of all believers, the lack of necessity for any mediating agent between human beings and Christ, the right of the Church to be involved in the world while not being captured by it, and the right of all believers to read and interpret the scriptures for themselves are still today the themes that define churches of the Reformed tradition. Luther, Calvin, and Knox helped to focus on these particular points through their writings and through the shaping of the Church in their respective countries. They felt that they were speaking the prophetic and apostolic Word of God into the present moment. They believed what they were saying in their historical settings to be a contemporary re-statement of what the prophets and the apostles had said in their own historical contexts. Thus, while the Reformed tradition does not claim that any of the Reformers were prophets in the Old Testament sense, it certainly claims for them *prophetic activity*, as that activity continued the prophetic message of the prophets of the biblical era. The Reformers were theologians who struggled to bring the scriptures of the Church into contact with their contemporary society, and who, having heard the Word of God as delivered by the Holy Spirit through scripture, then applied it in their day.

Today the traditions of the Reformed movement are most visible in the Presbyterian, the Reformed, and the Lutheran denominations. There are differences between these traditions at various points, and these traditions now stand at variance to some degree with the thinking of their various founders. Yet, the broad outlines of doctrine and of God's movement toward humanity are present within all of the denominations. As always they continue to struggle with the biblical witness to Jesus Christ as conveyed through the Old and New Testaments, and they continue to wrestle with the way in which that witness interfaces, informs, and corrects the contemporary Church and the society in which that Church exists. Thus, the Reformed tradition is always a *reforming* tradition. It is never complete. It is never final, for God continues to speak a new Word to his Church as the Holy Spirit enlivens scripture in each new setting in which the Church finds itself.

11

Reflections

What can one say of Joseph Smith? For most Mormons the answer is clear. Joseph Smith is a prophet of God in the same way in which Ezekiel, Jeremiah, Isaiah, and other Old Testament personages were prophets of God. Many Mormons would say that if that is not true, then the only alternative is that Joseph Smith was a fraud and a liar. But that is not the only necessary option. God has always used fallible human beings to accomplish his work, even though the efforts of those human beings have been far from perfect and far from complete. Without question, Joseph Smith was a fallible human being. He himself insisted (to the undercutting both of those who sought to messianize or deify him and of those who sought utterly to disparage him) that he was no more than an instrument of God. He never made messianic pretensions. His confessions are accompanied with the sober acknowledgement that he was "a man 'subject to passion,' and liable, without the assisting grace of the Savior to deviate from that perfect path in which all men are commanded to walk" (HC, Period I, Vol. 1, p. 10). Thus, the question before both Mormon Christians and Christians of other traditions is whether Joseph Smith, with all his human failings, was in fact used by God to bring about change within the Church of Jesus Christ.

The answer to that question can only be a personal answer. Out of faith the Mormon community has heard Christ calling it to the renewal and rededication of human lives which had found limited direction within the confines of the more established denominations. To such people, Joseph Smith is truly a prophet of God, for he has been the one through whom Mormons have heard Christ's call to renewal and commitment. Those outside the Mormon Church, who argue that the Mormon conception of Joseph Smith as prophet is in error, accomplish little in constructive dialogue, for they have not experienced the enlivening power of The Church of Jesus Christ of Latter-day Saints.

They have not experienced the fellowship that has led to the changes in lives and priorities that members of the Mormon church have experienced. Thus, they are ill-equipped to evaluate the religious experience of their brothers and sisters. To the Mormons, Joseph Smith is precisely whom they believe him to be—a prophet of God and of his Christ. Joseph Smith looked at an historical situation that seemed at variance with his understanding of the scriptures and of Christ's love for all, and raised his voice in opposition to such fragmentation of the Body of Christ. In that perception he was perfectly correct, but in responding to it, he added one more fragment in the eyes of those who stand outside the Mormon tradition. However, to Mormons, Joseph Smith restored Christ's unified Church at the Lord's command. That is their statement of faith.

Christians who are not Mormons have a more difficult time coming to grips with Joseph Smith. Clearly, they do not believe Smith to have been a prophet of God in the Old Testament sense. Many follow the easy path of simply claiming him to be a charlatan and a fraud. But this is a superficial evasion, for as one reads his writings, the fact that he was a deeply spiritual person and a deeply committed Christian comes through undeniably. Thus, what can a Christian who is not a Mormon say with regard to this religious leader of the nineteenth century?

First, one must recognize that he was a person who claimed Jesus Christ as Lord and Savior. Therefore, we are dealing with a Christian. He was also a person who was deeply concerned about the message he found in scripture and about how best to live out that message on a daily basis. He was a person deeply interested in questions of what happened to the twelve tribes of Israel, what was the origin of the American Indian, and what the relationship of Christ might have been to persons who did not live in Palestine in the first century. He answered these questions in the Book of Mormon and in his other writings. Some of his answers came through visionary experiences which we cannot explain, but which we must recognize as extremely important

13

to him. He bound his experiences and his questions into a theological whole that grew over time. The fact that he was untutored in a formal sense is to say nothing more than to say that Abraham Lincoln was untutored in the same way. Both had a thirst for knowledge. Both were self-taught. Both had minds that were curious about all things. Abraham Lincoln turned his self-learning toward shaping a nation. Joseph Smith turned his self-learning toward the shaping of a religious faith. Joseph Smith was probably a genius. He was certainly a theologian who sought to give life and vitality to the Christian experience as it met the various realities of frontier life. Certainly over the last 150 years, his writings and his teachings have given depth and meaning to the lives of people who have been touched by them. Granted, there are theological principles in his writings that are difficult for Christians who are not Mormons to accept. But theological principles are only the things which define the *traditions* to which we belong. This means that Joseph Smith was a Christian, but not of the Reformed or Roman Catholic traditions. He was a Christian of the Mormon tradition.

It seems that to claim that Christ cannot and has not used Joseph Smith and the denomination that Smith brought into being, would be to shut our eyes to the realities of what has happened within The Church of Jesus Christ of Latter-day Saints. It would also be a rather arrogant assumption to believe that Christ must operate through the channels that we establish, and cannot use other channels than the ones with which we are familiar. There should be no doubt that Joseph Smith was used by Christ. Likewise, there should be no doubt that Joseph Smith, like all people of faith, did not always accurately hear Christ speaking to him, and that he did not always accurately interpret scripture. Those differences we can quietly discuss with his followers—as Christian to Christian. But having said that, we should also be ready to kneel and worship with our brothers and sisters of the Mormon tradition, who follow the teachings of Joseph

Smith, an agent of Jesus Christ. Joseph Smith's role in the broad history of the American Church can be viewed in much the same way as the histories of Martin Luther, John Calvin, John Wesley, and John Knox in their own historical contexts.

"You Are Peter and On This Rock I Will Build My Church" Matthew 16:18

2

The Church of Jesus Christ of Latter-day Saints and Its Authority

There is perhaps no single word which more quickly separates Mormonism from other branches of the Christian Church than the word "authority." When a Mormon claims that the churches of today which are not Mormon are apostate, that individual is claiming that the proper channels of *authority* to implement Christ's directions and mandates no longer exist within the non-Mormon Christian structures. Churches other than The Church of Jesus Christ of Latter-day Saints do not bear Christ's authoritative priesthoods. Thus, they can never be full mediators of the gospel of Jesus Christ. This is the logical extension of Joseph Smith's vision of the Father and the Son in which he heard himself told not to join any of the existing denominations, for they were all incorrect.

Priesthoods

During the time that Joseph Smith and Oliver Cowdery worked on the translation of the Book of Mormon, they were forced to wrestle with a number of issues that related to the question of authority. In his history Joseph Smith states that in May of 1829, after working on a section of the

17

Book of Mormon that dealt with "baptism for the remission of sins," he and Cowdery went out into the woods to pray about the meaning of this phrase. Smith tells us that while in prayer a messenger from heaven descended upon them in a cloud of light, laid his hands upon them, and ordained them (JS-H 1:68) using the following words:

> "Upon you my fellow servants, in the name of Messiah, I confer the priesthood of Aaron, which holds the keys of the ministering of angels, and of the gospel of repentance, and of baptism by immersion for the remission of sins; and this shall never be taken away from the earth until the sons of Levi do offer again an offering unto the Lord in righteousness." (JS-H 1:69)

In this experience Smith says that the personage gave them the right to baptize others, and therefore Joseph baptized Cowdery, and then Cowdery baptized Joseph. This messenger identified himself as John the Baptist.

This event is significant, for it is the first step toward the establishment of a priesthood that is limited to The Church of Jesus Christ of Latter-day Saints. It is the first in a long series of events leading toward the restoration of things from the past which Smith believed to have been lost in the churches of his day. According to Mormonism, the Aaronic Priesthood is a preparatory priesthood, the priesthood of Elias, the schooling ministry, which prepares its worthy and faithful ministers for the oath and covenant of perfection which pertain to the Melchizedek order (D&C 84:15–40). Faith, repentance, and baptism are the outward ordinances which fall under the Aaronic Priesthood and which lead one to higher things. Those higher things are of a spiritual nature. Thus, the right to lay hands on other persons that they may receive the Holy Ghost is not something that is part of the rights of those who hold the Aaronic Priesthood—i.e., the priesthood Smith and Cowdery received in May of 1829.

Later, Joseph Smith states that he and Oliver Cowdery were once again visited by heavenly persons, but this time the persons were the Apostles Peter, James, and John. These three individuals conferred upon Smith and Cowdery the higher priesthood—i.e., the Melchizedek Priesthood. This priesthood had its origins in eternity prior to the creation of the world. In *Teachings*, Joseph Smith says, "It is the channel through which the Almighty commenced revealing his glory at the beginning of the creation and of this earth, and through which he has continued to reveal himself to the children of men to the present time, and through which he will make known his purposes to the end of time" (*Teachings*, pp. 166–67). This priesthood controls all things prior to creation, in creation, and in eternity following death.

The Melchizedek priesthood was in effect and present up until the time of Moses, and then was present, according to Joseph Smith, in the great prophets of the Old Testament. However, except for those periods of brilliance, the Melchizedek Priesthood was essentially withdrawn until the time of Jesus. In Christ, to whom the writer of Hebrews refers as the high priest forever after the order of Melchizedek, this holy and eternal order was once again spread upon the earth. His apostles were holders of the priesthood. After their death Smith believed that the priesthood of Melchizedek was not properly transmitted. However, it was restored once again, when he and Oliver Cowdery received it under the hands of Peter, James, and John.

One can more clearly understand the Mormon position that the Melchizedek Priesthood is absolutely essential to the proper ordering of Christ's Church here on earth, if one turns to another statement by Joseph Smith which says:

> "Some say the kingdom of God was not set up on the earth until the day of Pentecost, and that John did not preach the baptism of repentence for the remission of sins. But I say, in the name of the Lord, that the kingdom of God was set up on the earth from the days of Adam to the present time, whenever there has been a righteous man on earth unto whom God revealed his word and gave power and authority to minister to his

name. And where there is a priest of God—a minister who has power and authority from God to administer the ordinances of the gospel and officiate in the priesthood of God—there is the kingdom of God" (*Teachings*, p. 271).

This question of authority clearly sets the Mormons apart from other denominations within Christendom. It highlights as well the reason that Mormons feel compelled to evangelize not only non-Christians, but also their neighbors who are of other Christian traditions. The Mormon church holds that *Christ* has established certain authoritative channels through which his grace and the fullness of his gospel are mediated. Thus, even though Christians of other denominations read the scriptures and gain a knowledge of Jesus Christ, they cannot respond properly and totally to him. They have no one holding the proper keys to Christ's authority, as represented in the Aaronic and Melchizedek Priesthoods, to enable them to fulfill the ordinances of the gospel. Without access to that authority, the non-Mormon denominations have only a portion of the gospel and not its fullness. Therefore, Mormons proclaim the good news of the restored Church of Jesus Christ with its proper authority and keys not only to non-Christians, but also to their neighbors who are Christian. For those Mormons who truly understand the theology of their church, they make this proclamation to their neighbors, not in arrogance, but rather out of love and concern for them.

The focus of all church authority is found in the President or the Prophet of the Church. The President or the Prophet is the one person on earth who holds the keys to the kingdom of God in its fullness. He holds the keys to salvation itself, as it is made available to all Christians through the priesthoods. In actuality, he is viewed as God's spokesman upon the earth, and, thus, he is the earthly head of the kingdom of God. Therefore, the living Prophet according to Mormon belief is also a latter-day manifestation of the restoration of Christ's Church in all its authority.

The Organization of the Church

A Living Prophet. The Mormons believe that God has not only made known himself, his will, and his ways in Jesus Christ, but also that through Christ he established a pattern for the organization of his Church that should be present in all ages. This idea relates to the Mormon belief in the re-establishment of Christ's proper authority through the restored church. Thus, when one asks Mormons what the organization of Christ's Church should be like, they turn immediately to the scriptures of the Old and New Testaments. In the Mormon view, prophets were, and thus should always be, God's representatives in the world. They are the individuals who convey God's word to his people and who look into God's future for his people. The Mormon believes that when people seek the guidance of God on both temporal and spiritual issues, God's intent is that there be, in every age in which the true Church exists, a prophet who can convey God's will to his people. Thus, the first sign of the Church of Jesus Christ on earth is the presence of a living prophet who can give guidance to the Church. Today, that person in Mormon belief is Ezra Taft Benson of The Church of Jesus Christ of Latter-day Saints. He is one of the prophets in a succession of latter-day prophets since the time of Joseph Smith.

Twelve Apostles. Secondly, the Mormon church believes that Jesus established a quorum of twelve apostles to carry on his work following his death and resurrection. It is their belief that this group was intended by Christ to be present in every age as an organizing and guiding light to the Church as a whole. Mormons believe that in the first century, the apostles had worldwide authority to organize the work of the Church and to proclaim the gospel. As already noted, the Mormons claim that full apostolic authority disappeared with the death of the last apostle around 100 A.D., and that this group was never replaced or reconstituted. Therefore,

21

because the Church no longer had its guiding light, it fell into a period of struggle and partial light, until the year 1830 when the Church was restored to earth with its authority and its proper organization. Thus, as noted earlier, the restoration is evidence to Mormons that other denominations had become apostate.

The Seventy. Thirdly, the Mormon church notes that Jesus sent out a group of 70 individuals to preach his gospel (Luke 10:1). The presiding group, which exists below the level of the twelve apostles in the Mormon church, is a group called the Seventies. These persons have responsibility for regional areas of the church and the organization and the ongoing work of the church in those particular regions.

The Presiding Bishopric. Fourthly, the Bible indicates that there were persons primarily responsible for the temporal problems of human life such as hunger, poverty, and loss of one's spouse. In Acts 6:1–6 these persons were called deacons, and the Mormon church has established what is called the Presiding Bishopric to deal with the temporal issues of the church's life. Encompassed under the Presiding Bishopric are all of the relief programs, as well as the training and development of persons holding the Aaronic Priesthood.

The Broad Church. The names of all levels of the priesthood within the church are biblical. Within the Aaronic Priesthood are the office of deacon, teacher, priest, and bishop. The office of bishop, however, is held by a person of the Melchizedek Priesthood, and that person then is given responsibility to guide the work of the members of the Aaronic Priesthood. Within the Melchizedek Priesthood one finds the offices of elder, seventy, high priest, patriarch or evangelist, and apostle. Each office is an ordained calling established through the laying on of hands for service in a specified field of priestly responsibility.

Having noted that there are offices within the Aaronic and Melchizedek Priesthoods, we should also say that the priesthood transcends any of the offices. A person receives the Aaronic or Melchizedek Priesthood and then may be called to particular offices within it. By becoming a member of the Seventy, an elder does not gain more of the Melchizedek Priesthood, but rather only holds a different responsibility within the Priesthood. One cannot gain more "priesthood" by moving from one office to another office. An elder has all the priesthood he will ever need to stand before God and to serve him in the highest of celestial glories.

Yet, having said this, it should be noted that no one, not even the President of the Church, receives a fullness of the Melchizedek Priesthood except in the house of the Lord. This means that the ordinations to the Aaronic and Melchizedek Priesthoods and all the offices within them are but preliminary to this higher blessing which is the prerequisite of being able to stand before God in his celestial glory. It is thus that the distinction between priest and layman, or between priestess and laywoman, is finally erased. The vision of Moses will be fulfilled—all will be prophets. (See Joseph Fielding Smith, *The Improvement Era*, Vol. 73, June 1970, pp. 65–66.)

Men, Women, and the Priesthood. All male members of the church may be called to fill any of the offices within the Aaronic or Melchizedek Priesthoods. As a matter of fact, all male members are expected to move through the Aaronic Priesthood offices of deacon, teacher and priest, to the office of elder in the Melchizedek Priesthood. Therefore, all male members of the church are eligible for all offices within the priesthood. Thus, there is no "professional clergy" in the Mormon church, as there is in most other Christian denominations. There is truly a lay ministry among Latter-day Saints which involves all of the church's members. There is a high degree of organization, but also a high degree of equality in terms of the possibility for each person to hold the various offices.

Having said this, it must be noted that the Priesthood is held only by men. Women may hold offices within the Relief Society, but they do not hold the priesthood. It is the belief of the church that God has established a natural role for women in the home and in the family, with all the responsibilities for teaching, love, and support that are required within that context. Men, on the other hand, do not have a *natural* right to the priesthood. This is something that is given only as they demonstrate themselves to be *worthy* to hold it. In a sense, women hold by nature a unique office before God—that of wife, mother, and shaper of the home. By nature, men are not so privileged. They must earn their right to stand before God with divine responsibilities. Most Mormon women see this as God's divine plan. Most do not feel that they have been excluded from privileges that should be theirs. Most feel that as they participate in the church along with their husbands, who hold various offices of the priesthood, that they are contributing to the ongoing life in Christ's Church. There are some, however, who do not feel this way, but these women seem to be in the minority, since there are a myriad of ways for all persons to participate in responsible positions within the total life of the Mormon church.

For an interesting view into the life and roles of Mormon women, the reader might like to consult *Mormons and Women* (Santa Barbara: Butterfly Publishing, Inc., 1980) by Ann Terry, Marilyn Slaght-Griffin, and Elizabeth Terry. The Terrys are LDS and Slaght-Griffin is Presbyterian.

Perhaps the most graphic description of God's ultimate plan for women in Mormon thought is given by James E. Talmage.

> "In the restored church of Jesus Christ, the Holy Priesthood is conferred, as an individual bestowal, upon men only and this in accordance with the divine requirement. It is not given to woman to exercise the authority of the Priesthood independently; nevertheless, in the sacred endowments associated with the ordinances pertaining to the house of the Lord, woman shares with man the blessings of the Priesthood. When the frailties

and imperfections of mortality are left behind, in the glorified state of the blessed hereafter, husband and wife will administer in their respective stations, seeing and understanding alike, and co-operating to the full in the government in their family kingdom. Then shall woman be recompensed in rich measure for all the injustice that womanhood has endured in mortality. Then shall woman reign by Divine right, a queen in the resplendent realm of her glorified state, even as exalted man shall stand, priest and king unto the Most High God. Mortal eye cannot see nor mind comprehend the beauty, glory, and majesty of a righteous woman made perfect in the celestial kingdom of God." ("The Eternity of Sex," *Young Woman's Journal*, vol. 25, p. 602.)

Unity in Church and Life. There is probably no denomination within Christendom that binds its members more tightly together in the Christian daily life than does The Church of Jesus Christ of Latter-day Saints. If one were to diagram the relationship between the Church and the world in Mormon thought, one would draw a circle and label that circle "the church." Within the circle would be small compartments labeled recreation, school, politics, community service, sunday school, worship, etc. *All* of life is sacred. In contrast, most Catholics and mainline Protestants would draw a circle, but their circle would be labeled "life." Within that circle one would have compartments called recreation, politics, church, community, family, etc. True, their life within their church would hopefully inform their actions within other aspects of their lives, but "church" is only one compartment among many compartments. There is a line between things "sacred" and things "secular." Among a group of Mormons, conversation inevitably turns to the church, because that church encompasses all things. Among a group of Catholics or Protestants, rarely does conversation deal with the church outside of the church, for the many other demands upon the time and talents of these people tend to press the church into the background. Perhaps we of the Protestant and Catholic traditions should take a lesson from our Mormon neighbors and redraw our circles of life.

The Reformed Churches And Their Authority

Holy Scripture

In the Reformed tradition, scripture and the Holy Spirit stand at the center of all questions related to authority. Luther's battle cry "scripture alone" has permeated the life and thought of all Reformed traditions since 1517. Luther's dictum is aimed at a church which he felt oft times did not hear scripture, but rather, on the basis of tradition and history, established doctrines and practices that ran counter to scripture. His point was that all doctrines, all aspects of life, all political entities should be constantly checked against the scriptures. Thus, Church did not supersede scripture, but rather scripture, as enlivened by the Holy Spirit, stood above the Church. Hence, members of the Reformed tradition will turn to the authoritative witness of Jesus Christ which they find within the pages of Holy Scripture, for scripture is the one place where God authoritatively speaks his Word into the Church and into the contemporary world.

Prophets, Apostles, and Holy Spirit

It is this unswerving tie to scripture that leads the Reformed tradition to claim that it has a constant and living prophetic and apostolic witness in the Church and contemporary world. This claim is not based upon a continuity in hierarchy or a particular organizational structure. Rather, the Reformed tradition holds that the Holy Spirit is constantly operative in the interpretation of scripture, and is the one who brings a prophetic and apostolic message to the people of God. Therefore, authority is rooted in the Spirit of Christ, who makes alive once again the words of the prophets and apostles from the past. At the same time, the members of the Church are bearers of the Spirit. Thus, Christ's will and direction for the Church are manifest in the give and take of the community of faith, as that community wrestles with the content of scripture under the guidance of the Spirit. In the Presbyterian Church, if one asks what person he or she should go to for a definitive interpretation of a particular scriptural passage, the answer is, "There is no such *person.*" However, individuals are encouraged to study scriptural passages, examine them, and submit their understandings to other Christians who also bear the Spirit. Then, using the God-given intelligence that they possess, individuals seek to come to a deepened understanding of scripture in light of discussions with other Christians. This process affirms that the Spirit continually leads and draws *all* members of the Church to deeper and deeper understandings of God's ways and works all through life, and that when we believe we have reached a final and definitive answer on a theological question, we in actuality are closing our minds to the continual leading of Christ.

Individual Responsibility

Thus, within the Reformed tradition there is a high demand for intellectual and spiritual responsibility laid upon each person. Each is challenged to listen prayerfully and quietly to the guiding of the Spirit, as that Spirit leads one through Holy Scripture. Obviously, the first thing that the Spirit does is to lead individuals to personal relationships with Jesus Christ. Only then does the Spirit draw people to consider theological questions, to consider the mysteries of a God who became incarnate. To paraphrase St. Anselm's words, the Spirit leads people of faith to seek an understanding of the one in whom they have faith. Therefore, there is a constant ebb and flow of discussion, thought, and excitement within the Reformed tradition, for we are constantly discovering new things within the pages of scripture under the guidance of the Spirit as he works upon all of us in the Church. Through the scriptures God continues to reveal himself in Jesus Christ, as well as his will and his ways for his people.

Confessions

As Reformed Christians learn and relearn the lessons of scripture, they place those lessons into confessions or creedal statements. These are not substitutes for scripture (or should not be), nor are they finalized doctrinal stances to which all must subscribe. Rather, they are the results of persons in particular historical moments listening to the scriptures, and then recording, in the light of the particular historical circumstances, their understanding of God, his work, and his world. This God is made known only in Jesus Christ, who is revealed through the pages of scripture. The confessions (creeds) provide broad guidelines within which Reformed Christians read scripture, but at the same time scripture always challenges and checks the confessions. If there are things in the confessions which later generations discover to be contrary to the Word of God as revealed in scripture, those confessions are totally open to change and correction. Confessions are teachers and guidelines, never dictators. This is a fact that many Mormons may not understand about their Reformed Christian neighbors who use confessions within their church life. Confessions are far from the "abomination" which some Mormons conceive them to be. But rather they are the guiding lights of the church and the distillation of the Christian experiences of our forebears which we need to hear and from which we need to learn, but which we should never canonize or set in concrete. Mormons can trust the affirmation of Joseph Smith that the creeds contain truth but are not to be elevated to the status of Scripture or taken as final and closed formulations (Teachings, p. 327).

Organization

The churches of the Reformed tradition seek to ground their organizational patterns in the Bible, just as do the Mormons. They do not, however, try to reinstate all the varied offices of the early churches. Reformed Christians believe that organizational patterns are not divinely mandated, but rather arise from the varying needs of churches in unique historical settings.

Actually, the whole question of church organization drives us back to the exegesis of Matthew 16:13ff. Protestants and Catholics have wrestled with the meaning of this passage for centuries, and the Mormon church has added another voice and dimension to this same question. In the passage we see Jesus asking the disciples who they believe him to be. Many answers are given, but Peter finally says, "You are the Christ, the Son of the Living God." Jesus then responds, "Blessed are you Simon bar Jonah! Flesh and blood have not revealed this to you, but my Father who is in Heaven. And I tell you, you are Peter and on this rock I will build my Church and the powers of death shall not prevail against it. I will give you the keys of the Kingdom of heaven and whatever you bind on earth shall be bound in heaven and whatever you loose on earth shall be loosed in heaven." (RSV)

Discussions have always centered around the question, "Upon what is the Church founded?" Is it founded upon the person of Peter and his authority, which is then continued through an episcopal system, particularly in the office of Pope? Is it founded on revelation? Is it continued through the Melchizedek Priesthood, particularly in the office of Prophet, Seer, and Revelator? Or is the Church founded upon the confession of Peter that Jesus is the Christ, the Son of the Living God? Catholicism has traditionally claimed that the intent of Jesus was to establish a *hierarchy* in which Peter and the other episcopal leaders of the Church bore an authority over the Church and the world.

Mormons would claim that the Church is founded upon *revelation* which comes to an individual Mormon, as well as being mediated through the Prophet and the priesthood. It was by revelation, and not by "flesh and blood," that Peter recognized Jesus as the Christ. It was by revelation that Christ recognized Peter as a potential giant of faith and love. Mormons do not believe, any more than does the Reformed tradition, that God founds his Church on people—not even upon as great a person as Peter. But they do affirm that an organization resulted from the leadership, instructions, and ordinations of Jesus Christ.

Protestants have traditionally claimed that no hierarchy was established or intended in Jesus' words, but rather that the passage affirms that the Church is founded upon the *confession* that Jesus is the Christ, the Son of the living God. The Church as a *whole* is enlivened by Christ's Spirit and bears Christ's authority upon earth. How one interprets this particular passage of scripture says a great deal about how one understands Christ's authority to affect persons on earth and how one views organizational structures.

Because Presbyterians believe that the Church is founded upon Peter's confession and not upon Peter's person, and that Jesus mandated no specific offices or structures, they feel free to develop organizational structures that meet the needs of people in a given historical setting. They see the value of two basic biblical offices of elder and deacon, the former dealing with the spiritual and organizational matters of the Church and the latter dealing more with the human needs of persons (cf Acts 6:1–6). Presbyterians have a deep distrust of placing significant power in the hands of any one individual, and, thus, they use a representational form of government which demands that *groups* of people bearing Christ's Spirit make decisions for the Church. By doing so, they involve laity deeply in the Church's ministry, and the laity hold equal responsibility for ministry with the clergy, although particular callings may differ. Every person has his or her unique vocation within the total body of Christ, but no one has any special power in relationship to others.

In conclusion, the Church is Christ's universal body. It is made up of persons with varying gifts and varying vocational callings. But every individual is important due to the contributions that he or she can make. Thus, organization within the Church is designed to permit persons of varying skills and emotional levels to function as smoothly and completely within Christ's Universal Church as is possible. The Reformed tradition would claim that there was and is no established "right mode" of organization within the Church. Organization serves an end, but is not an end in itself. Christ works through *every* and *any* organizational structure within the confines of his Church. It matters little whether that organization is episcopal, organized around priesthoods, is based upon the laity, has a pope, has a prophet, or has neither. However, persons of the Reformed tradition believe that the organization which involves the broadest range of people in the life and ministry of the Church is the best for those who live within the Reformed boundaries.

Reflections

This chapter has dealt with the question of authority and with the problem of organization within the Church. But where does this authority lie? Whether persons are Roman Catholic Christians, Presbyterian Christians, Mormon Christians, Methodist Christians, or Eastern Orthodox Christians, all would confess that final authority in the Church lies with Jesus Christ himself. The discussion becomes clouded when an attempt is made to define how the authority and guidance of Christ come into the world and are applied within his Church. Mormon Christians claim that full authority and direction are to be found only within the authorized channels of the Aaronic and Melchizedek Priesthoods as restored in The Church of Jesus Christ of Latter-day Saints. Reformed Christians would claim that the full authority of Christ has been present from the conception of the Church and that it has never been lost. They would agree that at certain times the Church listened less responsively and responsibly to Christ's call than it did at other times in history. Nevertheless, because the Spirit of Christ *always* rested upon the Church, so also Christ and his authority were *always* present within the Church. Various people were called by God to provide correctives to the direction the Church was moving at given points in history, but total restoration was not needed—only revitalization and reformation. The Holy Spirit has provided ongoing continuity within Christ's Church from the day of Christ's resurrection until the present moment.

Are the Reformed and Mormon positions mutually exclusive? The answer from the Mormon perspective would be "yes," to some degree. While a Mormon would recognize that non-Mormon Christians reflect Christ's direction and goodness in their lives, that same Mormon would have to say that the fullness of the gospel and the authority of the priesthood do not exist within denominations apart from the Mormon church. However, Reformed Christians say that structures do not capture Christ's authority. Because the root of all authority in the Church is the Holy Spirit, then full authority can be found in many different organizational patterns. Thus, Christ is as authoritatively present in the episcopal structure of the Catholic Church, as he is in the representative structure of the Presbyterian Church. By extension, then, he is also equally present in the priesthood structure of the Mormon church. Christ uses our earthly organization to accomplish his heavenly ends, but is not bound or delimited by any of the organizations. And yet, each organization is of Christ's own making for he fitted the organization to the needs of his people—people who differ from one another in their emotional makeup and structural needs. People of Christ's Church are different from one another. People of the Church worship and express their faith differently from their neighbor. Thus, while denominational distinctions are a blot upon Christ's Universal Church, they are a product of human need, as well as of human sinfulness. Because we deal with sinful human beings, we can never hope for a totally unified Church in our time or in any future time. But we can hope that the Church will open itself to its religiously diverse components, so that all persons within the Church can come to an appreciation of the beauty, the authority, and the organization within which their Christian neighbors function. It is doubtful that Mormon Christians, because of their stress on the restoration of the Church in 1830, can accept the idea that full authority can exist beyond the boundaries of the priesthood. However, it should be possible for Reformed Christians, who have no such theological basis for segregation, to recognize that Christ's full authority lies within the priesthood traditions of their Mormon neighbors. Christ does not operate only where we would expect him to, nor does he operate as we might wish him to. God's ways are his own ways. Thank God that Christ is more gracious and more loving than we.

From our discussion, it is clear that for Reformed Christians there is unbroken continuity from the early Church to the present day. While aberrations have occurred, due to human sinfulness, in the history of the Church, there is still an ongoing wholeness to the life of the Church in which we of the current day continue to participate and continue to fulfill. However, the Mormon Christian believes that in about 100 A.D. something was lost, and in 1830 A.D. something was restored—i.e., Christ's authoritative priesthood. Unfortunately, this means that for the average Mormon Christian a knowledge of the thought, the scriptural interpretation, the organizational questions, and the questions about authority which circulated in much of the Church's life, is not part of their current thought structures. Mormon Christians should be encouraged to discover the richness of the Church's life between 100 A.D. and 1830 A.D. And while they will undoubtedly still hold that the true Church of Jesus Christ was restored in these latter days, they may come to a deeper appreciation of the faith which their Christian neighbors of other denominations hold and proclaim. Such knowledge and such a learning experience could be healthy for everyone concerned. Certainly bridges to understanding could be built much more easily without requiring anyone to give away the things which are important to their individual faith.

Finally, it should be noted that there is a distinct disjunction between the role of the church and the other aspects of life among average Protestants or Catholics. "Church" too often occupies a very small part of the Reformed Christian's life. Because of the stress on individual responsibility, on individual ability to read the scriptures, and on individual choice, the Church can become peripheral in the lives of Reformed Christians. Reformed Christians need to take a lesson from their Mormon Christian neighbors (who hold very similar beliefs on individual accountability and responsibility) about the place and role of church in the life of the true believer. Christ's Church can never be and should never be peripheral in the life of a person of faith. The Church must be and should be central. The Church should be exciting, dynamic, and fulfilling. Where this is not true, there is a real need for a new reforming movement. The Mormon church probably captures as fully as any other Christian body in existence today the excitement of the new life brought to them in Jesus Christ. We of other Christian traditions should not close our eyes to this fact. We should not act out of jealousy or negativism, but should simply rejoice that here is a lesson we can learn from our Mormon Christian neighbors.

"Go . . . and Make Disciples of All Nations" Matthew 28:19

3

Two by Two, The Missionaries Knock Upon Doors

A Preaching Mission

Most of us have at one time or another seen two young men in white shirts and ties walking or riding bicycles through our neighborhoods. Others have had these same young persons knock on our doors and offer to share their faith in Jesus Christ. These young men, and now many young women, are the missionaries of The Church of Jesus Christ of Latter-day Saints. They have one basic mission, and that is to preach the gospel of Jesus Christ to anyone who will listen. That "anyone" includes Christians of other denominations. Why? Because, as has already been said, the Mormon church believes that there is additional truth, beauty, and understanding to the gospel and an authority to the priesthood in the Mormon church that is not found in other Christian denominations. The compulsion to preach to all is a compulsion motivated by love for one's brothers and sisters. Anytime persons have something that is deeply meaningful to them, they seek others with whom they can share their experiences. So also with the message of the Christian gospel. The Mormons have heard very clearly Jesus' command to preach the gospel to all nations, and they believe that if they do not fulfill that demand, they are being less than the people Christ calls them to be. Therefore,

Mormon missionaries are to be found in all corners of the world preaching not only to non-Christian people, but also to Christian people in order that all might find the sense of fulfillment and commitment that the Latter-day Saints themselves have found within the Mormon church.

The Missionary Lessons

If a family consents to hear what the missionaries have to say, they will be asked to take a series of lessons, usually taught in their own home, detailing the basic precepts and principles involved in the Mormon faith. The family will be taught about a latter-day witness to Jesus Christ, about the apostasy of the Church, about the restoration of the Church in 1830, about Joseph Smith, and about the plan of salvation that God and his Christ have worked out for all people. If people smoke and/or drink alcoholic beverages, tea, or coffee, they will be taught the Word of Wisdom (D&C 89) which indicates that these practices are unhealthy for an individual. Since the body is the temple of the Holy Ghost, to pollute it with things which in any way alter it, is a violation of God's will for his people. To abstain from these elements is also an act of self-discipline, which then carries over into the everyday life of individuals, helping them to bring other aspects of their lives into balance. The potential convert will be challenged to read the Book of Mormon during the missionary lessons and to seek through prayer God's direction about the accuracy of its Christ-centered narrative and the claims of the church.

The Holy Spirit Converts

Those missionaries who truly understand the doctrine of their church know that they themselves are not the agent that opens the eyes of investigators to the truth of the gospel of Jesus Christ. Only the Holy Spirit does this. Thus, every missionary will challenge potential converts to kneel in prayer about the truth, or lack thereof, of the message that the missionaries preach and about the truth of the content of the Book of Mormon. The potential convert cannot help but appreciate the deep religious faith and sincerity of these young men and women, most of whom are between the ages of 19 and 23. It is exciting to find someone who is not afraid to discuss theology, and who actually has a thirst to do so. It is impressive to meet people so committed to Jesus Christ that they will give two years of their lives to missionary work, and whose families will provide the monies to enable them to preach the gospel in the farthest corners of the world. It is exciting to go to a sacrament meeting with the missionaries, to be greeted with outstretched hands and open arms, and suddenly to feel included in a vital part of the body of Christ, especially if one's own denomination has faltered in its educational and fellowship responsibilities. It does not take long for one to develop a testimony that Jesus Christ is truly present within this church, that he is most definitely proclaimed within the pages of the Book of Mormon, and that the lives of these people manifest him day by day. It does not take long to realize that the Holy Spirit can, in fact, lead people into this particular branch of Christ's Church!

Silent Witness

The missionary activity of the Mormon church is the primary mode of its efforts in evangelism, but evangelism is not limited solely to proclamation. Rather, there are distinct social ministries within the church which are viewed as evangelism in its broadest sense. Unfortunately, both Mormons and non-Mormons alike rarely hear of these ministries.

On a visit to Salt Lake City, I had the privilege of talking with a leader in the church. We talked about a number of things, but finally he began to reminisce about the years he had spent as a mission president in Southeast Asia. He was there shortly after the Vietnam War and the area was overflowing with refugees and boat people. People needed help in so many ways, particularly in relocation. Seeing the needs, the Mormon mission teams in that area, with the blessing of the church leadership, involved themselves in deeply humanitarian work, asking no questions about religious affiliation. They simply loved the people. When asked why this sort of ministry was not more widely known, the individual replied that somewhere in the New Testament there was the admonition that when one gave assistance to others, the right hand should not know what the left was doing. However, in saying this he did note that he felt the Mormon church could do better in their social and humanitarian responsibilities. Even so, the involvement is significant and growing. It should be noted that in 1983 the Mormon church began reducing the number of welfare projects it operates and reemphasized the importance of each member's responsibility for personal and family preparedness. One of the stated purposes was to free members for volunteer Christian service within their communities.

Sadly, there is a notion that Mormons help their own people and no one else, a notion that is in error. It is true that despite the church's best efforts, many needy are not reached, even though extensive Mormon resources and energies are expended outside the Church as well as within it. The late Mormon apostle Matthew Cowley contributed to and participated in Salvation Army efforts for precisely this reason—i.e., "They are reaching some we miss." On the issue of helping those beyond the church membership, the record is better than publicity would indicate. Bishops are instructed to extend welfare aid as needs arise with the crucial *proviso* that the persons, Mormon or not, be willing, with their families, to do all they can for themselves. The word "welfare" contrasts in Mormon terminology to its typical use in government programs. To the Mormon, welfare aid means merited aid, a lift back to one's own feet. One of its leading exponents, President Marion G. Romney, was once approached by an eager non-Mormon. "I understand your Church has a welfare program," he said. "Yes," the President replied, "and if you become one of us you can contribute to it."

Nearly half of the persons given temporary assistance in 1978 at the Welfare Square Storehouse in Salt Lake City were non-members. For those who come to Social Services for aid (temporary accommodations, food, clothing, counselling, employment), the issue is not church membership but need. "We never tell anyone we won't help. We never tell anyone we can't help." But "work for assistance" is an important principle.

Perhaps the most far-reaching effort to those beyond the church has been in the Philippines, Hong Kong, Mexico, third world countries, and other areas where health, sanitation, and personal hygiene, especially tuberculosis and cancer prevention, are desperately needed. Through fairs, radio programs, television, and newspapers, Mormon welfare service missionaries have reached hundreds of thousands. Crisis and emergency aid has been given by the church in Guatemala, Nicaragua, the South Seas. In the wake of World Wars I and II in western Europe and behind the Iron Curtain, at least 10 percent of those who were reached by such efforts (statistics have not been carefully kept) were in no way affiliated with the Mormon church. In the 1970's some 640 welfare projects, designed for the needy, have been extended abroad including Australia, England, Korea, and the Islands of the Pacific (Leonard J. Arrington, *The Mormon Experience*, pp. 276, 278–79).

One moving element of the welfare plan in Mormon history is help from those in need to others in greater need. Thus, for example, in the aftermath of World War II, Mormons in the Netherlands organized and cooperatively planted hundreds of acres of seed potatoes which were to be harvested to alleviate their own destitute condition. Their leaders asked them instead (though the Dutch were still on meager food rations) to contribute potatoes to the Germans. Fasting and praying that God would overcome government regulations forbidding food exports, the people found the necessary doors being opened. Seventy tons of potatoes were distributed at the rate of about 100 pounds per family in Hamburg, Berlin, and elsewhere. The next year the Dutch repeated this project and sent an additional 90 tons of potatoes to Germany. The "Love One Another" campaign expanded so that the Swedes aided the Finns, the Swiss the Austrians, and the Belgians the Germans (See William G. Hartley, "War and Peace and Dutch Potatoes," *Ensign*, July 8, 1978, pp. 19–23).

Recently, the Mormon Church held two fast Sundays in 1985, the entire proceeds of which were to go to the hungry in Ethiopia and other third world countries through non-Mormon agencies with proven records of service to people. The response was tremendous. There had been some concern that the people of the church would not respond as well to the needs of persons beyond the confines of the Mormon community as they normally would to Mormon needs. Such was not the case, for even little children came bringing their pennies, nickels, and dimes, so that they, too, might be involved in this witness of love to others. The final total for Ethiopian aid was 9.6 million dollars. Thus, though the social witness of the Mormons may not be widely broadcast, it is present at every level of the church.

Some Divisiveness

While one can admire the tremendous missionary zeal of the church, one can at the same time recognize that it occasionally creates problems for them. When a group of approximately 30,000 missionaries is knocking on doors across the world, there is a high potential for overzealousness among these young people. Occasionally one hears stories of the missionary who places his foot in the door, and then will not permit one to close it until he has been heard. One hears stories of missionaries who constantly hound a person, to the degree that the individual becomes extremely angry at the church. But these are exceptions rather than the rule. As young people, the missionaries tend to be very sensitive to and very supportive of the people whom they meet. The danger of the missionary effort does not lie so much with the overzealous missionary, as it does in the individual motivations for missionary work.

Every Christian who believes that God has called him or her to be an evangelist and a spokesperson for the good news, must ask the question, "Why do I preach the gospel to others?" If the answer is "To convert my neighbor to my way of thinking," then that person should take a long look at his or her motivation for ministry. Is evangelism nothing more than hanging a collection of scalps from one's belt? Is the function of the evangelism of the Church merely to help people "be like me"? Any missionary who approaches a prospective convert with that view will quickly be tagged as arrogant, aloof, and self-deceived. However, when persons share the things that have the deepest meaning to them with another human being, they are setting a proper pattern for evangelism, provided they share that deeply meaningful part of their lives out of *love* for their neighbor. Properly, the Mormon missionaries evangelize their fellow human beings because they have a deep love for them. They recognize the non-Mormon as a brother or sister before the non-Mormon ever hears the gospel, and thus, out of an already established relationship of love and respect, the missionary shares the good news of the gospel of Jesus Christ as he or she understands it. No one can fault that motivation. The Mormon missionary is trained, counseled and admonished by his or her own leaders not to evangelize from a stance of superiority or arrogance, but rather from one of humility and love.

Word and Deed The World Over

Calling in Christ's Name

Reformed Christians, also, have a deep commitment to proclaim the good news of God's presence with his people in Jesus Christ to anyone who will listen. In the Christian world, the message of Jesus Christ is kept before the community through the regular Sunday worship services within churches and the opportunities for learning in Christian education programs. Church members on an individual basis seek to invite their friends and neighbors, who are not already actively involved in another Christian community of faith, to accompany them to worship and Sunday School. Churches have struggled long and hard with the question of how best to mount an evangelism program within communities which are predominantly Christian in nature. Christians of the Reformed tradition see no need to bring persons from the Baptist tradition, the Catholic tradition, the Methodist tradition, or the Mormon tradition into their churches. Rather, they rejoice that Christ has called these people into his service as Catholics, Baptists, Methodists, and Mormons. Yet, there are many nominal Christians and many cultural Christians who are involved in no community of faith, in no worshipping community, in no Christian learning community. These are the people that one seeks to reach, so that their lives may be deepened and enriched. Some churches follow the Mormon example of going door to door in their evangelism programs. Others depend more upon their members to reach out to friends and neighbors on an individual basis.

Word and Deed

Reformed churches have strong evangelism programs, particularly as they seek to proclaim the gospel to non-Christian persons. Churches of the Reformed tradition have missionaries in all corners of the world, proclaiming the gospel of Jesus Christ to Buddhists, to Muslims, to Hindus, and to people of many other faiths. But there has been a strong tradition that evangelism is not a process that is carried out only through the spoken word. Rather, it is also something that happens through deeds. Thus, an integral part of establishing a worldwide program of evangelism has always involved the intentional building of

Christian schools, Christian hospitals, and involvement in Christian social action where people's rights are forgotten. Therefore, the first contact that non-Christians have with the Christian gospel may well be through a Christian hospital in which their child is treated for a disease that their own doctors have been unable to conquer. Non-Christians will be asked no questions about their religious affiliations, but will simply be accepted as children of God with a need that can and should be met by persons who are concerned for other persons. Through this kind of contact, a door is often opened which then enables a person to proclaim to these people God's love for them in Jesus Christ—a love which has made the nurses and the doctors of the hospital care about them, even though there are significant differences in religious faith. One never can know how the Holy Spirit works to bring people to a knowledge of God's love in Jesus Christ. And, of course, Reformed Christians, like Mormon Christians, in the end believe that the Holy Spirit is the one and only agent of conversion. We can be tools in his hands, but we do not open the eyes or the ears of persons to the good news of Jesus Christ. Only God can do that, and thus, we can love and we can support people knowing that God's purposes will inevitably be done.

Chapters of Tears

This is not to say, of course, that the history of mainline denominational evangelism has not had its faults and its chapters of tears, for it has. The Crusades were ostensibly military actions to free the Holy City of Jerusalem and to bring the members of the Muslim faith into the Christian fold. All too often they were little more than a ploy to get the barons of Europe to cease fighting against one another and to redirect their energies against a common foe. Thus, the Crusades may have been fought less for Jesus Christ, than they were for the political stability of Europe. Similarly, the Inquisitions in Spain and the witch hunts of New England are very unhappy chapters in the life of the

Church. Clearly the arrogance of human beings ran rampant, and the love of Christ was lost from the hearts of many. More recently American missionaries have been anything but helpful in many countries in which they have sought to evangelize the natives. They tied Christianity to the destruction of indigenous cultures, languages, and roots, all of which was unnecessary. As we read such sad chapters, we can hardly avoid wondering whether Christ really does use this fragile and fragmented Church of his. And yet, we do see changes in our world which could only have been wrought by the Holy Spirit. Therefore, we must confirm that Christ is alive and well, even though all Christians are very faulty servants.

Finally, it must be said that mainline denominations may have recently depended too much on deed and too little upon the proclaimed word. It is so easy to think that we are evangelizing by demonstrating our compassion, and yet, if that compassion is not coupled with a word which proclaims Jesus Christ as Lord of all, then the deed is little different from that carried out by a non-Christian humanist who shows deep compassion for his or her neighbor. Actions are truly Christian only when they are combined with the preached word, and we of the Reformed tradition, who have placed such a high premium on the proclaimed word, must remember that word and deed do, in fact, always go together.

Reflections

As just stated above, word and deed do go together. Reformed Christians could well re-learn from their Mormon neighbors that the one-on-one personal approach to the sharing of one's faith has been the cornerstone of the Christian Church from its inception. It is undoubtedly true that Reformed Christians need to structure stronger and better modes of evangelizing persons who are on the fringes of the Church or who are non-Christians. We cannot depend solely upon our good deeds or our Christian institutions. We must always remember to *proclaim* the good news of Jesus Christ no matter how Christian our actions may appear to us. On the other hand, many Mormon Christians may need to remember that evangelism is not solely a product of the proclaimed word, but can be enhanced by deeds that do not ask questions of denominational or religious affiliation.

On the issue of acceptance of persons different than we, a comment needs to be addressed to Mormon readers. Mormons need to hear clearly the deep hurt and even anger that many persons feel having grown up in "Mormon country" as non-Mormons. They feel excluded at best, and at worst discriminated against, snubbed, pressured, and rejected. Where there are such deep emotions, something had to trigger them, and Mormons should be willing to do some deep soul-searching. Error and prejudice do not lie solely in the non-Mormon quarter. Perhaps the most explicit example of Mormon arrogance of which I know personally occurred to a friend of mine who is a Presbyterian minister. He serves in a small town which is seventy-five percent Mormon. Presbyterians are historically ecumenical in nature, and, thus, after discovering that his congregation knew little about their Mormon neighbors and that they felt excluded, he decided to do something about the situation. He went to the local stake president to inquire about ways that they could get to know one another better and could assist their community to be stronger. After listening for a few moments, the president's response was, "If you don't like it here, you know what you can do. You can leave!" In any community of Christians such an attitude is unacceptable, but this is what many non-Mormons have experienced or at least *feel* they have experienced. Deeds and words of love and compassion should be extended to all persons regardless of religious or faith stances. To do so only opens the doors for the loving and supportive proclamation of the good news of Jesus Christ. Happily, those doors have begun to open in my friend's community, and long overdue relationships are beginning to develop.

Thus, in love, we should look to the element that is most common to evangelism among all Christians. That element is the fact that we all believe that the Holy Spirit is the agent of conversion. The Mormon missionaries ask people to pray about the truth of the message which they proclaim. The Reformed missionary asks people to do precisely the same, for each knows that only Christ's Spirit can lead people into the knowledge of Christ's Kingdom and of Christ's Lordship. Our golden tongues, our good deeds, and our evangelistic efforts can never be more than tools in the hands of Christ's Holy Spirit. If we truly believe that, then we do not ever have to attack a person of a different faith. All we need to do is to proclaim the message of Jesus Christ and then let the Holy Spirit do his work. How sad it is to see people who feel they must tear down another person's beliefs before they can replace them with what they perceive to be *the* truth. Those who feel that they must approach their religiously diverse neighbor in this manner are really persons who hold little faith in the reality of God's converting Spirit. Their actions say that they actually believe that *they* can convert, and that they must convert through negativism. But negativism has never produced anything good. Rather negativism coupled with human arrogance produced the Crusades, the Inquisitions, the witch hunts, and the ugly American missionary.

Knowledge that the Holy Spirit is the one who converts people to the Christian faith enables us to love and respect our religiously diverse neighbor. We can be friends with the Muslim, the Buddhist, the Catholic, the Mormon, the Presbyterian, the Methodist, and the Jew. We can learn from each. We can have our own spiritual horizons deepened and expanded. And we can share as brothers and sisters the very things that excite our souls and deepen our perceptions of life. We do not have to approach one another in antagonism. Rather, we can approach each other in love. Evangelism, under whatever banner, which does not believe this *is not Christian evangelism.*

Finally, we must believe that the Holy Spirit calls people to serve Christ where Christ wants them to serve him. If we believe that God answers prayer; if we believe that persons

may kneel in prayer seeking guidance about denominational affiliation; then we must also believe that God directs
them in their decisions. Thus, whatever the decisions, we
should *all* rejoice in them. If a person makes a decision to
serve Christ within the Methodist Church, the Presbyterian
Church, or the Mormon Church, that is not their decision
nor our decision. It is God's decision. Prayer is answered.
Vocations are given. Every part of Christ's Church is holy
and is under the Lordship of Jesus Christ. And so, let us
relax before the Holy Spirit. Let us rejoice in our diversity.
Let us celebrate our commonality. And let us fall on our
knees and worship together.

Part Two: What Do We Believe?

"I Am the Way, the Truth, and the Life" John 15:5

4

The Source of the Mormon Testimony

An Objective Basis

In Mormon thought, as in other Christian thought, Jesus stands as the objective center of all consideration about God. Even in his pre-existent state Christ was the High Priest forever. In Mormon understanding the priesthood appears to be similar to the New Testament concept of the eternal word of God or the Old Testament sense of the wisdom of God. The priesthood is the avenue through which God communicates knowledge about himself. Thus, Christ, as the firstborn Son of the Father, is the High Priest par excellence, for it is through him that the deepest and most profound understanding of God, his purposes, and his ways is gained. Similarly, Christ exercises a prophetic role which ties closely to his role as High Priest, for a prophet also speaks the will and ways of God. Therefore, Jesus Christ is the source of all knowledge about God. He is the channel through which knowledge of the will of God and the plan of God is gained.

One gains knowledge of Jesus Christ, and thus of God and his will, in two basic places. The first of these is scripture. For the Mormon, scripture encompasses both the Old and the New Testaments, as well as the Book of Mormon, the Doctrine and Covenants, and the Pearl of

Great Price. In these writings one, in concert with the church, seeks knowledge of God's purposes for human beings and God's will for daily life. But the church mediates the proper understanding of scripture through the authority of the priesthood. Christ utilizes the priesthood to provide the proper interpretation of scripture. Thus, one sees in the Mormon tradition the joining of scripture and tradition, much as is found in the Catholic Church. In the end, the church, its traditions, its apostles, and its prophet stand over and above scripture. The church and its traditions interpret the intent and meaning of scripture, and thus, lead the believer into right knowledge and correct understanding. Truth then becomes *propositional* truth. It is truth as discovered and mediated through the priesthood and through the church as guided by the Holy Spirit. Just as Jesus conveys direct knowledge about God, so also the church in its mediatorial role conveys firsthand knowledge of God.

It is through this objective knowledge of God and his work, conveyed by the church and the priesthood as they are rooted in Jesus Christ and the Holy Spirit, that the believers grow and are nurtured in their faith. The Mormon community is not asked to believe blindly. Anyone who has lived among Mormons knows that there is consistent and intensive theological discussion. All members view themselves as theologians, with the right to struggle and to explore what they see being made known to them through scripture, through the Holy Spirit, and through the priesthood. On issues of faith and life that are critical to life, they turn expectantly to the living prophet for guidance and direction. This does not mean that they cease to probe and investigate responsibly themselves; rather it reflects their belief that God will not leave his children without guidance, and that he "will surely reveal his will to his servants the prophets" (Amos 3:7).

A Subjective Basis

Thus, on the objective side, the Mormon gains a testimony of faith through understanding who Jesus Christ is, what Christ conveys in his life, teachings, and priesthood, and what is spoken by the prophet. But knowledge does not create a Christian. Rather, in the Mormon view, the real testimony of the Christian is rooted in an experience of Jesus Christ. This is not merely knowledge of the head, but is knowledge of the soul, planted there by the Holy Spirit. And when that act of the Spirit takes place, there is a burning in the bosom that cannot be shut away. Then the Mormon has a true testimony to his or her faith in Jesus Christ who is Prophet, Priest, and ultimately King over all creation.

The Source of the Reformed Testimony

An Objective Basis

For the Reformed Christian, Jesus Christ is absolutely central to every thought about God, the world, and humankind. There is absolutely nowhere that one can go to find out what God, the world, and human beings are really like apart from Jesus Christ. *Only* in him do we come to an understanding of who and what we actually are as people before God. And *only* in him do we come to an understanding of why God has created this world and what our role and function within it are. One cannot look at the natural world and discover God. One cannot find God through propositional philosophical constructs. The only place in which the divine may be found is in the person of Jesus Christ, for within him is the Truth. He is the Truth because he is God's self-revelation. In Christ we do not learn simply propositions about God, but rather we actually meet God face to face.

In Christ we discover something we didn't want to know—i.e., that we stand in radical opposition to our God. Christ shows us through his humility and obedience in his priestly work, the pride and arrogance in which we stand before God. Similarly, in his kingly work—i.e., in his exaltation and majesty—he shows us how far we have fallen into stupidity, inhumanity, dissipation, and anxiety. And finally, in his work as mediator, in his prophetic work, he shows us the light and truth of God, while simultaneously showing us our own falsehood as we exist in darkness, refusing to hear and to obey the Truth that we encounter in Jesus Christ. Thus, the Reformed Christian encounters Jesus Christ as prophet, priest, and king. But in Jesus Christ we actually meet the *totality* of God and the essence of God, so that revelation becomes a meeting of God face to face, not merely *knowledge* about God, his ways, and his works.

But where does one meet Jesus Christ? The battle cry of the Reformation, and particularly of Luther, was that it was only in scripture that one gained a knowledge of Jesus Christ. Scripture alone reveals to the Church its Lord and Master. Christ alone is the Truth, and the prophets and the apostles were uniquely inspired to proclaim him. Because God uniquely inspired the writers of the Old and New Testaments to bear witness to his ultimate work in which he came to human beings as a human being in Jesus Christ, the scriptures are the only place the Church can go, and the only place it needs to go, to discover all that is necessary about God, the world, and human beings *as they really are*. Thus, for Reformed Christians, the source of testimony about the Truth as seen in Jesus Christ is scripture. How do we know that the scriptures bear Jesus Christ to us? We know because the Holy Spirit, who inspired the writers originally, now inspires the readers and the hearers of scripture as they are brought into contact with the Lord who is revealed within the Bible's pages. The Holy Spirit, and only the Holy Spirit, enables us to meet Christ within the pages of the Bible. But this is not merely an individualistic encounter with the Lord. Rather, it is a community act, an act in which all Christians share with their neighbor the things about God, the world, and their fellow human beings that they have each discovered as they have looked into the eyes of Christ in the pages of Holy Scripture. Thus, the person of Christ, the scriptures, and the community of faith, are the avenues which the Reformed Christian travels to come to a relationship with his or her God. This means that God's self-revelation continues each moment of each day as he speaks his revelatory Word to his Church through individuals and groups.

The Subjective Side

But just as knowledge alone is insufficient for the Mormon, so also intellectual assent to the realities we discover in Jesus Christ is not enough for the Reformed Christian. There is a subjective side to the gospel message, and that is the joyful and obedient response of Christians in faith to a Lord who has already acted on behalf of sinful humanity. Faith is not necessarily a feeling, but it is always an act of obedience, of living, of joy, of compassion. Having met Jesus Christ, Christians can no longer live the same kind of life they have lived before. Thus, faith becomes an outgrowth of Christ's acceptance of all humanity and of their confrontation with him.

Reflections

Among both Mormon Christians and Reformed Christians, the Holy Spirit is the one and only agent that makes real the experience of Jesus Christ. In Mormonism the Spirit enlivens the scriptures, makes vital the traditions of the church, brings one into contact with the church's testimony of Jesus Christ, and creates the internal testimony of faith which is manifest in the experience of a burning bosom. Among Reformed Christians the Holy Spirit also brings people into contact with Christ, opens the scriptural references to him, creates the community of believers, and creates the joyful response of faith within the individual. Thus, there are significant parallels between the two traditions.

However, there does appear to be a difference between Mormon Christians and Reformed Christians on the issue of what "truth" is. Mormons tend to view it as propositional, doctrinal, and moral truth. Reformed Christians tend to view truth as the self-impartation of God. Truth is not propositions about God, but rather God himself. These divergent perceptions of truth also lead to a divergence in the way Mormon and other Christians understand knowledge to be channeled into the church. For the Mormon, because truth is propositional in nature, the channel of knowledge is the priesthood, with Christ standing at the head and the President of The Church of Jesus Christ of Latter-day Saints being his prophetic representative here on earth. Through this avenue will come many and glorious things related to God and his purposes that have not yet been revealed. But within the Reformed tradition, just as God is truth, so also is God the channel of knowledge, as we meet that God in Jesus Christ through the Holy Spirit. As we will see later, the differences between Reformed Christians and Mormon Christians in their perceptions of the Godhead enable the Reformed Christian to encounter the *totality* of God in both the Son and the Holy Spirit, while for the Mormon Christian both the Son and the Holy Ghost point to a reality beyond themselves in the person of the Father God with whom there may be ultimate reunion and face to face communion.

None of this is to imply that Reformed Christians do not also seek propositional truth, as they read the data of Jesus Christ. Nor is it to imply that Mormons cannot conceive of truth in its wholeness as being bound up in the person of Jesus Christ. Yet the differences of emphasis do exist, and they determine the way the Reformed and the Mormon Christians each approach the question of the knowledge of God.

"All Scripture   5
Is . . . Profitable
for Teaching"
2 Timothy 3:16

The Mormons and the Canon

The Book of Mormon

In Mormon thought the canon will always be open. As we have just seen, the Mormon holds that there are many truths that God has yet to reveal to his people. There are many things that God has yet to say about himself. There are many things that God wishes his people to know in the years ahead about his will and his purposes for the church, as well as for each individual life. The church should always be open to the hearing of those new words as they are conveyed through the priesthood and particularly through the living prophet. When those words come, they should be recorded in writing for future generations, that they, too, may have the benefit of their predecessors' experiences with their God. Because of this belief, the Mormons hold other documents than the Old and the New Testaments to be scriptural. Principal among these is the Book of Mormon, which is believed to be "another witness of Jesus Christ."

In the discussion of Joseph Smith and his visionary experiences, one of the things mentioned was the visit by the angel Moroni who showed Joseph where a book of metallic plates was hidden. These plates were said to contain the history of a people who lived on the western continent. Mormons believe the Book of Mormon to be a translation of those plates. According to the Book of Mormon, a man by the name of Lehi was called by God to leave Jerusalem with his family around 600 B.C. They traveled until they reached a great ocean, where the Lord directed them to build a boat to carry them to a new world. They arrived in that new world through God's guidance, landing in what is now South or Central America. Tensions developed between two of the sons of Lehi, namely between Nephi and Laman. Nephi was obedient to his father while Laman was not. Thus, those persons who followed Laman were cursed, while those who followed Nephi were blessed by God. The Book of Mormon principally contains the history of the continuing relationship between the Nephite people and the Lamanite people, running through the time of Christ's birth, death, and resurrection, and culminating in 421 A.D. with the ultimate destruction of the Nephites. Some descendants of the Lamanites are among the persons that we know today as the American Indians.

The Book of Mormon is much in the style of the deuteronomic history in the Old Testament. It records the social and political dynamics of the Nephite and Lamanite peoples. It details many explicit prophecies concerning the coming of Jesus Christ, as well as appearances by the Lord on the western continent to the Nephite people. In the Book of Mormon, Christ calls his disciples, much as he did in the New Testament. He establishes a church, and the people remain loyal to him and peace reigns among them until almost 200 A.D., when a final cultural breakdown begins. The book is named for the last great leader of the Nephite people, Mormon, and it is completed and hidden by Mormon's son, Moroni. Contained within the pages of the Book of Mormon, particularly in some of the earlier writings, are extended quotations from the Old Testament, particularly from Isaiah. This reflects the fact that Lehi was said to have brought a number of the Old Testament writings with him when he left Jerusalem in 600 B.C. The Book of Mormon is, then, the first of the additional writings which the Mormons hold to be sacred.

Excursus: The Book of Mormon and Isaiah

Many contemporary Old Testament scholars hold that the Book of Isaiah was not originally a complete work as we have it today. Rather, it is held that at least two, and probably three, principal writers were involved in its production. These judgments are based upon perceived differences in historical background, language, and style.

The first major portion (chapters 1–39) is ascribed to Isaiah of Jerusalem and for the most part records his oracles spoken during the time when Syria and Israel were threatening the southern kingdom of Judah (738–737 B.C.) and during the reign of Hezekiah (ca. 715–687 B.C.). However, when one comes to chapters 40–55, a wholly new situation confronts the reader. Jerusalem has fallen. The people are in exile. The note of doom in chapters 1–39 has turned to hope. Cyrus of Persia is seen as the potential deliverer of the Jews. Thus, the probable date of this Second Isaiah is 539 B.C. Finally, a third segment is seen and reflects a situation in which the refugees have returned to the land and have begun to pick up the pieces of life that their ancestors left behind. Third Isaiah is therefore to be found in chapters 56–66 and dated ca. 530–510 B.C.

As noted above, large segments of Isaiah are quoted in the Book of Mormon, for according to the text, Lehi brought with him certain Old Testament writings, among them Isaiah (cf. 1 Nephi 5:11–13). If Lehi left Jerusalem around 600 B.C., or at least before Jerusalem finally fell in 587 B.C., he could have brought with him Isaiah 1–39, for this would have been completed in the late 700's or early 600's B.C. We find portions of these chapters quoted in 2 Nephi 12–25 (cf. Isa. 2–14). However, in 1 Nephi 20–21 we find Isaiah 48–49 quoted. Further, 2 Nephi 2–8 reflects Isaiah 50–52:2, Mosiah

14 parallels Isaiah 53, and 3 Nephi 22 images Isaiah 54. If one holds the position of many contemporary Old Testament scholars that Isaiah 40–55 arose out of the period of the Babylonian exile, they clearly could not have been brought to the new world by a person in 600 B.C.

Many Christians reject the division of Isaiah sketched above, and hold Isaiah to be an integrated whole in which Isaiah of Jerusalem looked into the future, saw the exile, the release of the Jews under Cyrus, and the return to the land. Each reader will have to come to his or her own conclusions on this issue, and then apply those conclusions to the Book of Mormon and its personages. If one holds that there are at least three "Isaiahs" reflected in the Book of Isaiah, it is difficult to see how there can be an historical basis to the account of Lehi bringing the Book of Isaiah in its entirety to the new world. However, if one holds Isaiah of Jerusalem to have been looking 150 years into the future, this particular problem is resolved.

Additional Scriptures

In addition to the Book of Mormon, there are writings which have been brought together and titled Doctrine and Covenants. These are primarily revelations given to Joseph Smith during his lifetime which have shaped the life, doctrine, and thought of The Church of Jesus Christ of Latter-day Saints. Included within the Doctrine and Covenants are also revelations given by Brigham Young, Joseph F. Smith, Wilford Woodruff, and most recently by Spencer W. Kimball. It is at this point that the Mormon canon is most visibly still open, for revelations through the living prophet can always be included in this collection of writings.

There is finally a small collection of writings known as the Pearl of Great Price. This contains selections from the Book of Moses, which is an extract from the Book of Genesis as Joseph Smith interpreted it under inspiration. There is also the Book of Abraham, which is an interpretation of some Egyptian papyri that came into the hands of Joseph Smith in 1835 and which Mormons believe to contain the writings of the patriarch Abraham. Further, there is a sample of Joseph Smith's interpretation of a portion of the gospel of Matthew, which like the Book of Moses was interpreted under divine inspiration. Finally, there is a portion of Joseph Smith's history, which tells about his initial experiences with God and the angel Moroni. The Pearl of Great Price ends with the Articles of Faith of The Church of Jesus Christ of Latter-day Saints.

These four standard works—the Bible, the Book of Mormon, the Doctrine & Covenants, and the Pearl of Great Price—constitute the scriptural foundation for The Church of Jesus Christ of Latter-day Saints. All doctrines of the church are rooted in these scriptures. But more than that, one quickly discovers that all doctrines of the Mormon church are first rooted in the scriptures of the Old and New Testaments. Each doctrine of the church is a product of the confrontation of its people with the Bible. One may not always agree with the way a scriptural passage is interpreted, but one must recognize that the doctrines of the Mormon church never arise from thin air with no reference to biblical sources. Joseph Smith was deeply immersed in the scriptures of the Old and New Testaments, and he was particularly drawn, it would seem, to Isaiah, Matthew, John, Hebrews, and Paul. Other biblical writings that appear to have left an indelible impression on him are the deuteronomic history, Daniel, Acts, and the Book of Revelation. These writings provided the seedbed for the fertile theological mind of Joseph Smith. Whatever else one may say about him, Joseph Smith was a man of the Bible.

Canon in the Reformed Church

Within the Reformed tradition the canon is viewed as closed—i.e., there will be no further additions to the literary corpus. This is principally because the Reformed tradition understands the canon to bear witness to the *once-for-all* act of God coming to his people in Jesus Christ. Thus, the canon of scripture is God's witness to his eternal intent to dwell with his people in Jesus Christ. Scripture is not a creation of the Church as it learns new propositional truths about God over time. There is nothing more that can be said about God than can be revealed through the pages of scripture, which bear witness to God's real presence among his people. God's personal coming is a one-time act. Therefore, God inspired the writers of the Old Testament to look toward the time when he would dwell with his people as the "Emmanuel," as the "God with us." He likewise inspired his witnesses in the New Testament to look back at the one-time event of the incarnation when he came to dwell with his people as a human being. Thus, both the Old and the New Testaments are oriented toward precisely the same event, the event of the incarnation. Therefore, the content of the canon is God's content, God's witness to his self-revelation in Jesus Christ.

Christians are tempted to think that the *Church* has decided what is to be in the canon, but in reality all it has done is to confirm where it has heard God speaking to it across the ages. Reformed Christians believe that the canon is closed, because they believe God has closed it. All of our statements about God and about his Son are now rooted in his single unified witness to himself in the pages of scripture. Through those pages, God continues to make himself known by the power of his Spirit as the Spirit calls us again and again to new encounters with the risen Christ.

For the Reformed Christian, the focal point of the canonical literature is Jesus Christ. He is the *center* of the canon. The Old Testament moves toward him in expectation, and thus bears witness to him *in expectation*. The New Testament witnesses to him *in retrospect*. In essence, the content of the Old and New Testaments is the same—Jesus Christ. The Old Testament expects God with man, the Emmanuel, but is unclear about the way in which God will dwell with his people. The New Testament, on the other hand, is very clear about the way in which God has come to humanity, and stands in awe and amazement before the reality of the incarnate God who entered our world as a human being in Jesus Christ. Thus, both Testaments present Jesus Christ to every person who reads the Testaments under the guidance of the Holy Spirit. Hence, as all Christians read the Bible, they are confronted with Jesus Christ. These people then spend the rest of their lives letting their faith seek an understanding of the one in whom we all believe. It is this process of faith seeking understanding that is the process of theology, the process of reasoning about God based on his self-revelation in Christ and witnessed to by scripture.

Reflections

Joseph Smith and the Book of Mormon

For the Mormon, the Book of Mormon is precisely what Joseph Smith and his successors have said it to be. It is a history of a branch of the chosen people located on the American Continents and spanning the time from 600 B.C. to 421 A.D. It came from the translation of plates found in the hill Cumorah in upstate New York near the community of Palmyra. Joseph Smith was the one who carried out that translation. The Mormons have clearly heard Jesus Christ speaking to them from the pages of the Book of Mormon, and in their minds there is no question that it is another witness to Jesus Christ.

Other persons, not of the Mormon faith, have claimed that the book is a pious fraud, that it has no spiritual value, and that no non-Mormon can have anything to do with it. However, just as non-Mormon Christians can discover a common ground that enables them to appreciate more deeply Joseph Smith's contributions to the religious life of the Church, so also those same non-Mormon Christians may be able to find a ground that enables them to appreciate the Book of Mormon and its contributions to the Christian lives of the Mormon people. To evaluate the Book of Mormon, one really has to read it. In doing so, it becomes evident immediately that Jesus Christ is proclaimed as Lord and Saviour, and as the one who will come to lead his people

63

to freedom before God. Chapter after chapter attests to this fact. What then are we to make of this book, if we do not believe that it is in fact the history of a people on the western continent?

My personal answer is that the Book of Mormon stands as a monument to the faith of Joseph Smith, and reflects his deep immersion in the scriptural literature, as well as his struggle to understand the origin of the American Indians and the fate of the ten lost tribes of Israel. The book is not, I believe, a pious hoax, but rather the product of the visionary experiences of Joseph Smith that we can neither fully comprehend nor explain away. It is most definitely a witness to Jesus Christ, and it is a witness in much the same way that the theological works of Martin Luther, John Calvin, and John Wesley are witnesses to Jesus Christ. They are all based upon the scriptural message about Jesus, and they all seek to understand him more completely, and to articulate what they have discovered in him. So also is the Book of Mormon a compendium of Joseph Smith's theological wrestlings with Jesus Christ and the scriptural witness to him. Here Joseph Smith's derivative witness to Christ is not written in the form of a systematic theology, but rather is written as story and parable. It is a profound book. It should not be slighted in the study of American religious traditions. It should not be scoffed at by the uninitiated and the uninformed. The Book of Mormon should be appraised for what it claims to be, another witness to Jesus Christ, and with the understanding that it is Joseph Smith's unique witness to Jesus Christ, based upon a scriptural witness found in the Old and New Testaments.

The above answer will not satisfy a Mormon, nor should it. What we seek here is to deepen the understanding and appreciation of the non-Mormon for their Mormon Christian neighbors. Only the Holy Spirit can determine what is scripture for one person and what is scripture for another. From the evidences of the Spirit's activity within the Mormon church, we have to believe that that same Spirit takes the Book of Mormon and makes it scripture for his people within the Mormon Christian tradition. We of the

Reformed Christian tradition do not hear Christ's words in the same way within the Book of Mormon as do our Mormon Christian neighbors, but we can certainly read the book and appreciate it as a profound Christ-centered theological document, among the many profound theological documents to be found within the Church of Jesus Christ.

The Implications of Open and Closed Canon

The concept of open canon, as present within the Mormon tradition, points toward a concept of revelation which focuses on the will, the acts, and the purposes of God in the present and in the future. God always has a new revelatory word to speak which must be captured for future generations, thus necessitating an open canon. The concept of a closed canon, however, implies that God has given all he can give—that is himself. He may expand our understanding of that self-giving, but he cannot give *more* than he already has. That self-giving informs past, present and future. Thus, we may write theologies, but we do not need to nor can we write new scripture.

Our view of canon also dictates to some degree our understanding of Christology. If we understand the canon as still open, then we are more prone to view Christ as revelator, in the sense that he conveys *knowledge* about the past, the present, and the future. If we view the canon as essentially closed, then we will tend to view Christ as the *self-revelation* of God, capturing the past, the present, and the future in his person. The open canon tends to lead toward a conveyance of knowledge. The closed canon tends to lead toward a new relationship between God and humanity that is not totally dependent upon one's knowledge.

This canonical question also leads us to consider once more the Confessions (or creeds) of the Church. Mormons hold that God speaks periodically a new revelatory word into history, and therefore, there needs to be a vehicle, such as the Doctrine and Covenants, to capture this new sense of purpose and mission that comes from on high. Likewise, Christians of the Reformed tradition believe that God continues to speak his *one* revelatory word, Jesus Christ, into each new historical situation, and that Christ constantly calls us to new types of *responses* to these new historical situations. In the light of Christ's calling and the scriptural witness to him, the Church periodically writes what we call "confessions" to deal theologically with these new historical situations. In the best judgment of the Church at a given point in history and under the guidance of the Holy Spirit, a confession is the Church's statement of what it sees God calling it to be and to do in a particular historical moment. We collect these statements in a *Book of Confessions*, and we continue to refer to them and to learn from them. We do not canonize them as new scripture. Yet, they are a record of Christ's continued call to be responsive to and responsible for our historical lives. In function, is this not what the Doctrine and Covenants means in Mormon religious life? Need the Mormon castigate the Catholic or Protestant for having confessions, and need the Protestant or Catholic castigate the Mormon for claiming an open canon, when in fact we are doing essentially the same thing, but simply under a different name? Are we not perhaps making literary mountains out of semantic molehills?

From the standpoint of both Reformed and Mormon Christians, it should be possible to confess that we share a common scriptural foundation—the Old and the New Testaments. We differ on how and where Christ continues to speak to us within the context of our individual traditions, but neither of us doubts that he continues to speak. We need not deny that there are different theological perceptions that we hold based upon our reading of scripture, but need those divide us when, in fact, we worship a common Lord? Are not the real differences that we experience a product of the way in which we read scripture and interpret certain definable and identifiable passages? If so, then we have a basis for common discussion on common issues, based on a common source—the biblical witness to Jesus Christ. Perhaps the most productive path is to celebrate our commonality, while at the same time rejoicing in the diversity that can lead to a deepening and enriching of the faith of us all.

"In the Beginning Was the Word . . . and the Word Was Made Flesh and Dwelt Among Us" John 1:1, 14

6

With this chapter we begin the exploration of the basic theological precepts of both the Mormon and the Reformed traditions. Here we will begin to see some differences in the way in which God is conceived and some differences in the way in which God's plans are put into operation. Those who wish to explore the validity of any of these doctrines, whether they be stated with reference to Mormon theology or Reformed theology, must do so on the basis of scripture. We should never battle over doctrines. Rather, we should sit quietly together and mutually explore the content of Holy Scripture for the betterment of us all. From scripture we arrive at our individual doctrinal stances, and it is upon the basis of Bible study that we should be able to expand the horizons of one another. Once again, hostile confrontation creates nothing that is good, but prayerful and loving cooperation and conversation generate a much healthier body of Christ.

The Mormons and Jesus Christ

Pre-existence and the Trinity

God the Father.   Mormon tradition holds that there is one God and only one God with whom humans must deal. That

God is the God to whom the biblical literature bears witness, and Christians know that God as the Father. Mormons take very seriously the language of the Bible which speaks of God in anthropomorphic terms—i.e., in language which indicates that God has hands, feet, speaks, walks in the garden in the cool of the evening, and permits Moses to see his back. Thus, Mormons believe God the Father has a body of flesh and bones as do we, and we are created in God's image in a literal, physical sense. To those who would deny the physical nature of the Father, Mormons respond that this should be no more difficult to believe than the Catholic and Protestant position that the Son, who is the second person of the Trinity and one in essence with the Father and the Holy Spirit, becomes incarnate and in his resurrection is physically raised to the right hand of the Father without losing his truly human, physical nature. If Catholic and Protestant theologians can claim this reality for the Son, based upon scripture, then argue Mormon theologians, why is it so unthinkable for the Father to possess a glorified body?

When asked how the Father attained this body, the Mormon answer is that the Father of us all was a being as we are in a prior world. In his life in another world and in his life following his physical death in that world, our Father God grew in knowledge, wisdom, and intelligence to the point at which he was called to be the Celestial Father, or God, of his own world. We will look more deeply at this process in the next chapter when we deal with the doctrine of eternal progression. Suffice it to say at this juncture, however, that this is the only point in Mormon theology where there is a latent polytheism. There are, in Mormon thought, many gods who are celestial parents of their own worlds, but there does not seem to be an answer to the question, "Where and with whom did it all start?" Ultimately, this must be an unanswerable question. But even with this latent polytheism, Mormons are fundamentally monotheistic, because they deal with only one God, and he is the Father spoken of in the pages of Holy Scripture. While one may speculate about the existence of this God prior to his existence as our God, one can and will have no dealings with any other being than this one. However, the two aspects of God the Father that are made possible by his prior existence in another world are, first, his body of flesh and bones, and secondly, the beginnings of his celestial family.

A Celestial Family and Plan. As will be noted again later, the family is the fundamental unit of Mormonism. This family unit passes from this life into the next and family relationships continue. Parents continue to have children in the next life, but these are spirit children. Thus, our Father God, and by extension his wife, continued to nurture their family toward their exalted and eternal existence in the afterlife. The firstborn of their spirit children was Jehovah, who ultimately became known to us in this life as Jesus. Reflecting upon the biblical literature, the Mormons hold that the name of God the Father is Elohim, and that it was Elohim through Jehovah who created the heavens and the earth.

When the Father made the decision to provide the opportunity to his spirit children to advance like himself, he called a heavenly council to present his plan for salvation. It was proposed that his spirit children would go to earth, gain bodies of flesh and bones, be tried and tested in all things, and gain a knowledge of good and evil. They would be given the opportunity to exercise free choice and through their obedience would be given the opportunity to return to the presence of the Father. It was also explained that the Father would choose a redeemer to work out an infinite and eternal atonement on behalf of his children, and he asked who would be willing to fill that role. Two mighty spirits volunteered. The first was Jehovah, Christ, or Jesus. He embraced God's plan and affirmed that he would direct all glory to the Father. The second was Lucifer, but he sought to amend God's plan. He advocated compulsion and proposed to redeem all of humankind so that not even one soul would be lost. He then would take God's honor for himself. When the Father chose Jehovah to fulfill the plan of salvation and not

Lucifer, Lucifer, in pride and wrath, rebelled, led a third of the spirits against God, and was cast out of heaven. As a result of the council, God the Father proceeded with his plan, created the earth, and began to populate it by placing Adam and Eve in the Garden of Eden (see Moses 4:1–4, Abraham 3:25–28, D&C 29:36–40). This story of human progression will be continued in the next chapter.

Father and Son

It was necessary to tell this story of the pre-existence and the Father's history, so that the relationship between the Father and the Son in Mormon theology may be seen clearly. Mormons take extremely seriously the monotheistic language of the Bible. There is only *one* God, and that is the God of the Old Testament—the God who is known as the Father of Jesus in the New Testament. Therefore, while all of the attributes of deity are ascribed to Jesus and all of the creative acts of God are ascribed to him, there is still a subordinationism in his relationship to the Father God. Jesus, or Jehovah, is the firstborn of the Father. He stands in a uniquely close relationship to the Father. The Father's will and his will are one, and yet Father and Son are two distinct, unique beings. The Father and the Son, along with the Holy Ghost, who is also a distinct and unique personage—a spirit person—constitute the Trinity. Thus, the Mormon conception of the Trinity, or the Godhead, involves one God (the Father) along with two other subordinate personages, the Son and the Holy Ghost—but they are all one in purpose, design, goal, mission, and objective. The implications, then, of this conception of the Trinity for God's relationship to human beings are significant. *The one God does not actually enter our human sphere.* Rather his *firstborn son*, who bears all of the attributes of deity, does so. But there still remains a distance between the Father God and his human children, until such a time as those children have passed through the trials of earthly life and gained the knowledge and experience that will lead them back into the presence of the Father and reunite them with him.

Jesus' Role

What then is Jesus' role in this plan? Very simply, through his sacrificial and atoning death, he opens the door that leads to possible reunification between the Father God and his children who have taken on earthly life. Jesus can act on our behalf because he is completely like us in all ways. Both he and we are literal spirit children of a common Father, the only difference being that he is the firstborn and kept his first estate in such a manner that he was highly exalted in the presence of the Father. He entered our existence and took upon himself a body of flesh and bones just as we do. The difference between Jesus and us lies in the fact that Jesus was born of a virgin and his conception took place through the Holy Ghost. Thus, Jesus is the literal firstborn son of the Father in the pre-existence, the Only Begotten in the flesh, and the literal son of the virgin Mary in this life—the Holy Ghost being the agent of his conception (Alma 7:10). Further, Jesus was tempted as are we (Heb. 2:18), and he was utterly obedient to his Father and to his Father's plan as he went to his death on the cross to fulfill the plan of salvation. On the cross he voluntarily died for he uniquely had power to lay down his life and take it up again, and through the resurrection he is now glorified with the Father as a being of flesh and bones. So through him we may also be glorified. In his earthly life, Jesus taught us God's plan of salvation and served as an example of one who is utterly obedient to the Father. He lived a perfect life, and thus he could also be a perfect sacrifice in his atoning suffering and death.

The Atonement

The atonement of Christ is completely central to all Mormon thought. As we have already said, the Father's plan in the pre-existence demands that Jesus come and die an atoning death for humankind. Thus, how some ex-Mormons and other Christians can claim that there is no atonement in

Mormon theology is difficult to understand. Some quotations are clearly in order here.

Nothing in the entire plan of salvation compares in anyway in importance with that most transcendent of all events, the atoning sacrifice of our Lord. It is the most important single thing that has ever occurred in the entire history of creative things; it is the rock foundation upon which the Gospel and all other things rest. Indeed all "things which pertain to our religion are only appendages to it," the Prophet said. (Teachings, p. 121)

And this is the gospel, the glad tidings, which the voice out of the heavens bore record unto us—that he came into the world, even Jesus, to be crucified for the world, and to bear the sins of the world, and to sanctify the world, and to cleanse it from all unrighteousness; that through him all might be saved whom the Father had put into his power and made by him. (D&C 76:40–42)

Wherefore, redemption cometh in and through the Holy Messiah, for he is full of grace and truth. Behold, he offereth himself a sacrifice for sin, to answer the ends of the law, unto all those who have a broken heart and contrite spirit; and unto none else can the ends of the law be answered. Wherefore, how great the importance to make these things known unto the inhabitants of the earth, that they may know that there is no flesh that can dwell in the presence of God, save it be through the merits, and mercy, and grace of the Holy Messiah, who layeth down his life according to the flesh, and taketh it again by the power of the Spirit, that he may bring to pass the resurrection of the dead, being the first that should rise. Wherefore, he is the firstfruits unto God, inasmuch as he shall make intercession for all the children of men; and they that believe in him shall be saved. (2 Nephi 2:6–9)

. . . as in Adam, or by nature, they fall, even so the blood of Christ atoneth for their sins. And moreover, I say unto you, that there shall be no other name given nor any other way nor means whereby salvation can come unto the children of men, only in and through the name of Christ, the Lord Omnipotent. (Mosiah 3:16–17)

Many more passages could be cited, but these should suffice to demonstrate the centrality of the atonement in Mormon thought. Christ's death and resurrection free human beings from the curse of death brought upon them through Adam's sin. In Jesus' death immortality is given to all, but not necessarily exaltation. As will be seen more fully later, the things we do as human beings and our obedience to the Lord do determine how we stand before him in relation to our fellow human beings. But it is neither works nor obedience which determines whether people are released from the sins which lead to death. This is determined solely by Christ's sacrifice. Had Christ never died, all persons would dwell eternally in outer darkness with no hope of ever entering the presence of God. This is what Christ's life and death accomplish. This is the Mormon doctrine of the atonement.

Following his resurrection, Jesus returned to the presence of the Father, and dwelt with the Father as a glorified and resurrected being with a body of flesh and bones like his Father. Thus, Mormon thought holds that within the Godhead there now exist two beings of glorified flesh and bones—the Father and the Son—and one spiritual being, the Holy Ghost. Yet Jesus continues to be with his people on earth. First, his presence is made known through the Holy Ghost, the third person of the Godhead. Secondly, he is present through the light of Christ (as distinct from the Holy Ghost) which is the universal power through which God remains in control of all things. And thirdly, Christ is constantly with his people through the Melchizedek Priesthood of The Church of Jesus Christ of Latter-day Saints. Humankind is not left alone in the post-crucifixion and post-resurrection era. God has provided means of constant contact between himself and his Son and his people on earth through the Holy Ghost, the light of Christ and the Melchizedek Priesthood, particularly as that priesthood is made manifest in the living prophet. Thus, Christ's light is not limited to Mormons. Jesus Christ lights *all* people, manifests himself clearly to *all*, and his light grows brighter and brighter as he draws people ever closer to himself. (D&C 50 and 88)

The Reformed Tradition and Jesus Christ

The Godhead

When one turns to the Reformed tradition, there is no real necessity to deal with a pre-existence in the sense that Mormon theology does. The only eternally pre-existent being is God himself, and by definition God has existed from all eternity, with nothing existing prior to him. He has remained the same from all eternity. Thus, in revealing himself in Jesus Christ, God gives us *himself*, and thereby a unique *Christian* knowledge about himself. When we meet God in Jesus Christ, we discover that God is triune in nature. He is three persons—Father, Son, and Holy Spirit— while at the same time being one in essence. Reformed theologians bow before the mystery of this trinitarian God who is one, but who is also three persons in *one essence*, because they hold that the scriptures lead to this conclusion. It is clear that the scriptures affirm one God. But at the same time it is also clear that the Son and the Spirit are spoken of in precisely the same exalted language and given the same worship that the Father receives. (See, for example, Jn 1:1–14, 20:28; Heb 1:8; Rev 1:8; Matt 28:19; Phil 2:5ff.) Reformed theology, with its roots in the Catholic Church, affirms that we are confronted with a mystery that the human mind is incapable of comprehending. Therefore, we bow in a doxology before the mystery of the Godhead, which is infinite in character, inexpressible in finite language, and incomprehensible by the finite minds of human beings.

This means that the entire Godhead was active in creation, although one can speak of the Father as the primary agent of creation. This also means that the entire Godhead is active in the reconciliation of the world, even though one can speak of the Son as the primary agent of reconciliation. Further, it states that one can speak of the entire Godhead as being active in the redemptive or sanctifying process of humanity, while at the same time affirming that the primary agent of redemption is the Holy Spirit. This is the way God is, has been, and always will be.

The Incarnation

In the light of God's oneness in essence, when Reformed theologians speak of the Son becoming incarnate and entering human history, they are saying that *God* has actually entered human history. The God of the entire created universe is so great that he can become small, taking on the humanity of his creatures and meeting his creature face to face as a human being. Both the magnificence and the condescension of God are to be found in the beautiful and profound passage in Philippians 2:5–11.

> Have this mind among yourselves which you have in Christ Jesus who, though he was in the form of God, did not count equality with God, a thing to be grasped, but emptied himself, taking the form of a servant, being born in the likeness of men. And being found in human form, he humbled himself and became obedient unto death, even death on cross. Therefore God has highly exalted him and bestowed on him the name which is above every name, that at the name of Jesus, every knee shall bow, in heaven and on earth and under the earth, and every tongue confess that Jesus Christ is Lord, to the glory of God the Father.

Reformed theologians affirm the reality of the virgin birth, in which the Holy Spirit overshadowed Mary, impregnated her, thus permitting her to give birth to the God-Man Jesus Christ. Jesus is wholly and totally God, and is also wholly and totally human. Basic theological errors occur when persons fail to realize that both Jesus' humanity and divinity must be affirmed. The doctrine of the virgin birth does precisely this. Many persons err when they claim that Jesus was wholly God, but only *appeared* to be human and extraordinarily close to God, but was not the full penetration of the divine into human history and existence. If God's intent were to bring himself and humankind together in Jesus Christ, then in Jesus Christ God must dwell with humanity and humanity must be found with God. In the incarnation, God chooses to dwell with human beings *as a human being*. In the cross, human beings try one last time to rid themselves of the God who would meddle in their lives. However, in the resurrection God affirms that he will not leave his creature alone nor permit his creature to thwart his divine and eternal purpose to be with his people. In the transfiguration and the resurrection Jesus is shown to be Lord and King over all the earth, as he was in his inner-trinitarian existence prior to creation. He remains constantly and always with his Church through the Holy Spirit. He continues to guide and to lead it, so that its members and all persons of all nations may dwell fully in the presence of God for all eternity. God is, thus, very close, very personal, very real in the lives of his people. He is not distant.

Reflections

As we look back on the two expositions of the Trinity, we see the Mormon tradition maintaining the oneness and personal character of God by focusing on the Father as the one God. We also see that oneness maintained, with its character of three persons—Father, Son, and Holy Ghost—by the stress on oneness in *purpose* between the members of the Godhead. When we turn to the Reformed tradition, we find the oneness of God, as stressed in the Old Testament, continued. Yet, at the same time, we see the statement, as Reformed theologians look at Jesus Christ, that God is one with three persons of *one essence* within himself. How this can actually be, the Reformed theologian cannot grasp intellectually, nor can anyone define this mystery in limited human language or thought forms. Rather, the Reformed tradition bows in praise and doxology before a mystery that it cannot wholly comprehend. It can only affirm the oneness of God in three persons of one essence, due to the fact that it finds this witness within the pages of scripture.

When one turns to scripture, it must be admitted that nowhere is the doctrine of the Trinity, as stated in the Reformed tradition, made explicit. Rather, the theologians of the Catholic and Protestant churches have affirmed that this is the logical extension of the language of the Bible and of what they learn of God as he reveals himself in Jesus Christ. Mormon theologians, on the other hand, claim that the language of the Bible is clear and to be accepted precisely as it appears. They understand the Bible to state that there is one God—the Father—and that the Son and the Holy Ghost are subordinate to him. Their oneness is a *functional* oneness, a oneness of purpose. This position is not far distant from that held by the Eastern Orthodox traditions. The very question of whether the Father and the Son were of the same *essence* is part of the reason that the eastern and western branches of the Church ultimately separated from one another in 1054 A.D.

In concluding our discussion of the Trinity, it must be affirmed that both the Mormon and Reformed traditions claim that God is one, but that he is also three. The fundamental difference occurs over the issue of whether the Godhead is one in essence or one in purpose. For those who hold that God is one in essence, when the Son becomes incarnate God in his wholeness has truly entered human history. For those who hold that God is one in purpose, when the Son becomes incarnate the majesty of the Godhead enters human history, but not the essence of the one God. In the Reformed tradition, then, God already dwells in his fullness with his people in this age, both through the Son and the Spirit, even when his children do not recognize that fact. In Mormon tradition, God will dwell totally with his children who attain celestial exaltation, but this will occur only after their resurrection. This is not to say that he leaves them alone or without comfort in this life, but it is to say that God the Father has not approached humankind in quite the same way that Reformed theology understands God to have approached his human children.

Finally, any discussion of the Trinity is actually a discussion about God's presence with his people. The Mormon stress on the continuity between the Father and his children from pre-existence through exaltation underlies the closeness and personal relationship that exist between God and us. God the Father is close, personal, compassionate, and familiar. Precisely the same sense is conveyed to persons of the Reformed tradition as they talk about the Father, Son, and Holy Spirit as *persons*. God is present, near, and personal as he meets us as creator, reconciler, and redeemer. Mormons sometimes hear the Church's traditional language which exalts God's greatness and infinity, but they miss the language of closeness and nearness that the doctrine of the Trinity provides. Traditional trinitarian language praises God's constant and personal presence with his people.

Even with the theological differences focused around the nature of God, it is safe to say that within both the Reformed and the Mormon traditions, Jesus by his atoning death bridges the gulf that exists between God and his creature. Once again, human intellect cannot totally capture how this has occurred, and thus even the Bible uses a number of forms of imagery to try to explain the inexplicable. The Bible talks in juridical language, in sacrificial language, and in relational language. All point to the mystery of God freeing humanity from its arrogance, its sloth, and its degradation, so that all persons might have fellowship with God. The locus of this freedom is to be found in the atoning death of Jesus Christ.

Coupled with the atonement in both traditions is the assertion that by his obedience and his resurrection Christ is revealed as being the one who reigns over us for all eternity. In Mormon thought, there is a certain sense of newness to Christ's post-resurrection reign. While Christ was the supreme exalted being in the pre-existence, he has now *grown* and *progressed* through obedience and the acquisition of a body of flesh and bones, thereby becoming like his exalted and glorified Father. In Reformed thought, this sense of change or progression is unnecessary, for in the incarnation the Son did not acquire any new attributes or powers. Rather, he remained the eternal Son who was with the

Father from eternity, and continues to be the eternal Son who reigns with the Father and the Holy Spirit into all eternity. The only difference is that now in Jesus Christ *humanity* dwells totally and completely with God. God now sees all of his children caught up in the humanity of Jesus Christ, and thus true humanity—humanity as God created it to be—dwells in God's presence.

"I Came From the 7 Father and . . . Again, I Am . . . Going to the Father" John 16:28

The Mormons and Eternal Progression

First Parents

We have already talked about God's announcement to the Heavenly Council of his plan to enable his spirit children to have the privilege of advancing like himself. It was a plan of grace and love, according to Mormon thought, which would enable persons to take on physical bodies, experience the challenges of good and evil, to gain knowledge, and to have a family relationship with spouse and children. It would be necessary for Jehovah or Jesus to die an atoning death to free humanity from the fall of Adam and Eve for which the Father planned and prepared. Through the atoning death of Christ, the possibility of entering the celestial glory in the presence of the Father would be open to all people, with certain provisions. The plan was put into effect, and the archangel Michael was the first spirit child of God to enter this earthly realm as Adam and to take on a physical body (D&C 27:11).

However, Mormons hold that while he was in the garden, Adam was still immortal. He was a being of flesh and bones, but not being of flesh and blood, the latter signifying mortality while the former state signifies immortality. In his immortal state Adam could not experience death, corruption, or procreation. Thus, God had planned that the fall occur, so that Adam and his successors might truly be able to follow the path of eternal progression which God had laid before them. Therefore, God permitted the temptation of Adam and Eve which led to their fall, and thus directly to the possibility that they might attain the glory for which they were created by their Father. Once having fallen, Adam introduced mortality and death into the earthly existence. But more importantly, he enabled all of his descendents to have the right of free choice, the ability to gain knowledge, the responsibility of deciding between good and evil, and the ability to reproduce themselves, thereby providing physical bodies for the pre-existent spirits who were awaiting their opportunity to enter onto the path of eternal progression.

Adam was the first earthly being to hold the Melchizedek Priesthood, and from the time of Adam to Moses that priesthood was present upon the earth. The calling of Israel was for the purpose of setting aside persons to be a unique witness to God's plan and purpose, as was the calling of the Nephites on the western continent. Throughout the Old Testament literature, Mormon scholars see implicit references to Jesus Christ that are somewhat shaded and shadowed by the language and circumstances of that time. However, when one turns to the Book of Mormon, in the period from 600 B.C. until the coming of Christ, there are many explicit prophetic statements which proclaim Christ's coming and the purpose of his coming. Christ will free humankind from the temporal and spiritual death wrought by Adam's sin, and thereby open the avenue to the next stage on the path of eternal progression to all of those who prove themselves to be obedient to the Father's will. This will is made known through the prophets of the Old Testament and the prophets of the Nephite people. With Christ's coming, the people of God gained deeper knowledge and insight into God's will and purposes. This knowledge and insight should inspire them to obedience, if they truly hear the gospel through the medium of the priesthood, through the lips of a living prophet, and through those who serve God under the prophet's guidance.

The Family

One of God's principal expectations for humankind is that they will form family units in which children may be raised. The family unit is the central unit in Mormonism, and it is the place to which pre-existent spirits come so that they may enter earthly bodies. Many people have wondered why Mormons have such large families when there is a population explosion that is threatening the well-being of us all. The Mormon response to that question is that over-population on earth is not the real problem, but rather it is the over-population of heaven that must in obedience be addressed. The Father seeks to provide opportunity for all of his spirit children to enter onto the path of eternal progression, which requires that they take on human bodies and human experience. The more children a family has, the more spirits are released for participation in the Father's gracious plan. Because Mormons hold that they understand more fully and more completely God's purposes and plans, the spirit which enters into a Mormon household is already further along the path of eternal progression than is the spirit which enters a household that is not Mormon. Even though the non-Mormon household may be a Christian home, there is still "more to Mormonism," particularly as represented in the authority and priesthoods of the Mormon church. In these the non-Mormon does not participate, and may, in fact, never discover their reality in this life. Thus, whatever a Mormon family can do to provide opportunities for the spirits to enter this life within the context of a family which belongs to the restored church is all to the good. The parents believe that if they are obedient by having children, God will provide for them and for their family, and that they are really not contributing to a world-wide problem of over-population. This life is the necessary prelude and preparation for the next life.

Eternal Progression

Arising from the belief that this life is preparatory to the next and provides an opportunity to choose between good and evil, there is a significant optimism in Mormon thought about the ability of human beings to make right choices under the guidance of the Holy Spirit. It was an optimism shared by many religious thinkers in the 19th century, both in this country and in Europe. There was a real confidence that human beings were in control of their own destinies, albeit with the guidance of God, and that they could and would make choices that would lead the world to evolve toward a better end than was present at any given moment. In America, this optimism was to some degree a product of frontier self-sufficiency, which led people to believe that there were few obstacles they could not confront and conquer, if they were but given the materials and the time to do so. Thus, mortal existence in Mormon thought is the time in which decisions are made and human beings gain knowledge and wisdom, all of which may lead them into the celestial glory of the Father God. In this life men and women are constantly progressing in their knowledge of God and in their obedience to that same God.

This process does not cease at the time of death in Mormon thought. The Mormon can never conceive of a static existence before God without continued growth, knowledge, and responsibility. Thus, the process of eternal progression involves implicit gradations in spiritual and intellectual life in the next existence, just as there are observable gradations in the spiritual and intellectual lives of persons in this existence. Even God continues to progress and grow in the glorification of his children. Even he is not static. Before we react too negatively to the concept that God thus changes, we should remember that in many Protestant and Catholic seminaries today classes are being taught on *process* theology. The fundamental principle seems to be that, because we can see and observe change in this world created by God, there must be a continuity between his created order and his being, thus implying that God is also a God who grows and changes. While it is not at all clear why one must necessarily infer a changing God from a changing created order, it is worth noting that the concept of a God who progresses in this sense is not unique to Mormon thought.

Freedom of the Will

Throughout the history of the Christian Church, theologians have constantly discussed the relationship between divine grace and human freedom. The answers that have been formulated cover the spectrum. Some claim God's call is irresistible—all are saved. Others hold that God opens a tiny window in a person's soul that allows that individual freedom of choice and responsibility. Still others argue that if there is not total human freedom to choose or reject God, then there can be no real love or relationship between God and humankind. It is the latter position that best reflects Mormon thought. Human freedom is part of uncreated intelligence. Thus, God's omnipotence is qualified, and the atoning act of Jesus Christ is not a final and irresistible cause. It is, instead, the definitive act to which persons may respond or not respond. People are genuinely free, genuinely responsible, and therefore genuinely capable of meritorious response or demonic rejection. Thus, God needs to act in a manner that will most powerfully influence his human children to a response of love. God yearns for humanity to become like him. He yearns to share all that he has and all that he is. This movement of God to us is his grace, and such a grace it is! It is grace powerful enough to turn a worm into a divine being like one's heavenly Father—but only if one fully accepts and fully responds to that Father. This is precisely the position to which most of Christendom ascribes. God offers salvation, but for it to be effective, we must respond in faith. To do otherwise brings God's judgment upon those who reject the gracious and loving offer.

Degrees of Glory

One finds the logical extension of eternal progression in the Mormon concept of three levels of heaven—the celestial, the terrestrial, and the telestial. As with all other doctrines in Mormon thought, this doctrine has its roots in scripture. In I Corinthians 15:35–42 (RSV) one reads the following:

> But someone will ask, "How are the dead raised? With what kind of body do they come?" You foolish man! What you sow does not come to life unless it dies. And what you sow is not the body which is to be, but a bare kernel, perhaps of wheat or of some other grain. But God gives it a body as He has chosen, and to each kind of seed its own body. For not all flesh is alike, but there is one kind for men, another for the animals, another for birds, and another for fish. There are celestial bodies and there are terrestial bodies; but the glory of the celestial is one, and the glory of the terrestial is another. There is one glory of the sun, and another glory of the moon, and another glory of the stars; for star differs from star in glory. So it is with the resurrection of the dead. What is sown is perishable, what is raised is imperishable.

The Mormons understand this passage to state that there are differing physical bodies in the resurrection. Just as there are in nature heavenly bodies, earthly bodies, and bodies like the stars, all of which differ in glory, so also one can expect celestial, terrestrial, and telestial resurrection bodies. If there are these three bodies, then clearly, the Mormon believes, there are also three levels of glory after death in which God places the majority of humankind. It is these degrees of glory which Christ has opened to persons across the face of the earth, and were it not for his atoning sacrifice, no person would ever be able to proceed on the path of eternal progression or to experience the joy of life after death. Persons find their initial niche in this tripartite heavenly structure based on the degree of maturity and on the level of response they have given to the properly proclaimed gospel of Jesus Christ.

Celestial Glory

All persons who have accepted Christ and been obedient to him—that is, had faith in him, repented of their sins, been baptized by one having the authority of Christ to baptize, received the Holy Ghost through the laying on of hands by one holding the Melchizedek Priesthood, and subsequently been obedient to God's callings and commands—will enter into the celestial kingdom. This kingdom is ruled over by God the Father and Jesus the Son. The inhabitants of this kingdom will enjoy the full glory of God, as they continue to grow in wisdom and knowledge and responsibility. For those who have entered into the bond of celestial marriage, meaning that they have been sealed in the temple for time and eternity, there is the possibility that they may be called at some point in their progression to be celestial parents of their own world and to populate it as God, their Father, populated this world. In a word, there is the potential for some celestially exalted beings to become gods with all the attendant responsibilities. (D&C 76:50–70)

There is also one other group of persons who may enjoy the celestial heaven. This group is made up of persons who did not have the opportunity in their earthly existence to hear the gospel of Jesus Christ proclaimed with its proper authority and proper content, but who accepted it in the afterlife when it was preached to them. These are persons who would have rejoiced in the gospel in their earthly life, had they had the opportunity to hear it. This doctrine provides the Mormon answer to the eternal question, "What happens to persons who never have the opportunity to hear the gospel in this life?" (D&C 137:7–8). As we shall see in the next chapter, the full participation of these persons in the celestial glory rests in a measure upon the vicarious acts of relatives for them in the temple here on earth.

Terrestrial Glory

The terrestrial kingdom will be inherited by persons who led honorable lives in this life, by persons who died apart from the law of God, and by persons who rejected the gospel in their temporal existence, but who then accepted it after death when it was proclaimed to them (D&C 76:71–80).

Telestial Glory

Finally, the telestial kingdom is occupied by virtually all other persons. In D&C 76:99–112, it states:

> For these are they who are of Paul, and of Apollos, and of Cephas. These are they who say they are some of one and some of another—some of Christ and some of John, and some of Moses, and some of Elias, and some of Esaias, and some of Isaiah, and some of Enoch; But received not the gospel, neither the testimony of Jesus, neither the prophets, neither the everlasting covenant.
>
> Last of all, these all are they who will not be gathered with the saints, to be caught up unto the church of the Firstborn, and received into the cloud. These are they who are liars, and sorcerers, and adulterers, and whoremongers, and whosoever loves and makes a lie. These are they who suffer the wrath of God on earth. These are they who suffer the vengeance of eternal fire. These are they who are cast down to hell and suffer the wrath of Almighty God, until the fulness of times, when Christ shall have subdued all enemies under his feet, and shall have perfected his work; When he shall deliver up the kingdom, and present it unto the Father, spotless, saying: I have overcome and have trodden the wine-press alone, even the wine-press of the fierceness of the wrath of Almighty God. Then shall he be crowned with the crown of his glory, to sit on the throne of his power to reign forever and ever.
>
> But behold, and lo, we saw the glory and the inhabitants of the telestial world, that they were as innumerable as the stars in the firmament of heaven, or as the sand upon the seashore; And heard the voice of the Lord saying: These all shall bow the knee, and every

tongue shall confess to him who sits upon the throne forever and ever: For they shall be judged according to their works, and every man shall receive according to his own works, his own dominion, in the mansions which are prepared; And they shall be servants of the Most High; but where God and Christ dwell they cannot come, worlds without end.

Given the three degrees of heavenly glory, salvation is almost universal in Mormon thought. Following the second resurrection, the only individuals who will ultimately be banished to outer darkness are Satan, his angels, and a few others. It is not that Christ will have slammed the door against these "others." Rather, they will have slammed the door against him. The Mormon understanding is that only those persons who stand in the glory of the noonday sun and deny its shining will finally end in perdition or outer darkness. This is simply the logical extension of what has been said earlier about the Mormon understanding of freedom. Freedom is really freedom and can defy God forever.

Christ's atoning death is extremely broad. Even the telestial glory will be beyond human comprehension, and one need not sorrow for those who occupy it, except in the sense that the terrestrial and celestial glories far exceed the experience that those who inhabit the telestial kingdom will ever comprehend or know.

Within each of these three heavenly kingdoms, persons will continue to grow and progress eternally. Perhaps, and Mormons await further clarification, a person may move from one degree of glory to another—i.e., a person may move from the terrestrial kingdom to the celestial or from the telestial to the terrestrial. However, most current thought holds that once one is located in any one of the heavens, the person will enjoy the fruits of that level of heaven for all eternity.

A movement from pre-existence to earthly life to celestial glory—this Mormons understand to be the gracious plan of God stated in the Heavenly Council prior to the creation of the earth. This is why the Mormons are deeply obedient to the call of their God as they understand it and comprehend it. Their obedience is an act of faith, which God calls them to exercise as they grow in knowledge and wisdom, and as they progress in this life and in the next for all eternity.

The Inner-Trinitarian Decree and Reformed Faith

God's Purpose for Humanity

When members of the Reformed tradition seek an answer to what God's intent is for humankind, there is only one place that they can go to discover the answer to their question. That place is to Jesus Christ, the source of all knowledge about God, because he *is* God incarnate. As indicated earlier, in Jesus Christ the Church discovers an unique Christian fact about God—i.e., the one God is Father, Son, and Holy Spirit. The Church also learns, as an extension of that fact, that God's eternal purpose has been to dwell with his people as a human being.

It has been traditional in the theology of the Church to view salvation history as a process in which God continually seeks his people through the prophets of the Old Testament. The people proved to be stubborn and arrogant, and were constantly turning away from him and were in flight from him. Finally, after numerous attempts on God's part to reconcile himself to humankind, and after numerous rejections on the part of humanity of God's graciousness and God's approach, God decided upon a final, gracious act in which he would send his Son to redeem humanity and bring oneness between himself and them. He sent his Son Jesus Christ who died on the cross, and thereby worked a reconciliation which had not been possible prior to his earthly presence.

To some theologians, the God portrayed in this traditional salvation history appears as a weak, almost incompetent being. The supposed almighty creator of the universe is boxed into a corner by his creatures who are so arrogant and apparently so powerful, that God can do nothing but send, as a last gasp attempt, his Son to bring about a renewed relationship between himself and his errant children. True, his act is one of love, but it is an act of desperation and weakness, not an act that is thought out and planned ahead of time.

But is this the only way one can look at God's purposes? Was his intent in sending the Son to send a paramedic who would finally place a bandaid on a long-festering sore that had been unhealable? The answer is "no." This is not the only way to look at salvation history, especially when attention is turned to what can be discovered in Jesus Christ. If people believe, as does the Reformed tradition, that Jesus Christ is *wholly* God and *wholly* man, then they see that God dwells with humankind in the person of Jesus Christ. Thus, the Old Testament expectation that God will dwell with his people, that he will come as the Emmanuel—which in Hebrew means "with us is God"—is fulfilled in a very surprising way. God does not come on the clouds as the Lord of history with all his majesty and all his power. Rather, he enters history as a baby in a manger and is with his people as one human being to other human beings. Was this act necessitated by human sin, or was it God's intent from all eternity to be with his people in this manner? If God is all-knowing and all-powerful, then the only logical conclusion is that this was God's *intent* from all eternity. Thus, the Church is able to look back prior to creation into the inner-trinitarian life of God himself, and see the purpose of all history.

When the Church takes this look into the inner-trinitarian life of God, as it is made visible in his self-revelation in Jesus Christ, what is learned? The Church already knew that God existed as a relational being—i.e., as the Father and the Son bound together in the perfect love of the Holy Spirit. God was complete within himself and needed nothing outside of himself, and yet out of his incredible graciousness *he* elected to permit a being outside of himself to have a relationship with him. More than that, God would establish that relationship by becoming a human being himself, entering human existence as the Son, and thus relating to his children in love as one human being to another. Therefore, the emphasis in this theology shifts from the cross and the resurrection, from Good Friday and Easter, to the incarnation—to Christmas, when God fulfilled his eternal decree to dwell with his creature.

Creation and the Body

In order that God might fulfill his eternal purpose to be with his children as a person, he first needed a stage upon which this event could take place. Therefore, he created the earth, the animals, the vegetation, and in essence "laid the table" for his supreme creatures, man and woman. In Reformed theology, there is no belief in a pre-existence, for Gen. 2:4b ff is clear that man like the animals is a creature of the dust. In the Genesis narrative God is represented as shaping man from the dust of the earth, and only then breathing the breath of life into his nostrils, thereby making him a living, animated being. The human body is not a tabernacle for a pre-existent spirit. Rather, the human body is God's creation and it is good, but it is totally dependent upon the breath of God to sustain it. Should that breath be withdrawn at any moment, the creature would return to the dust and to separation from God. Thus, the earth and sheol were conceived as the place of the dead, the grave, in which there was no relationship with God. Human beings come from dust and return to dust. And, yet, it is precisely this creature with whom God has determined to have a unique relationship.

The Fall

The Reformed understanding of the fall is that it was a product of Adam's and Eve's temporal free choice and of their abject disobedience to God's commands not to eat the fruit of the tree in the garden. Prior to the fall, Reformed tradition believes that human beings had free choice, complete humanity, total mortality, and the ability to procreate.

In the pre-fall state humanity was created to dwell in the presence of God and in a close relationship with him, but Adam and Eve chose to shatter that relationship and to attempt to become gods themselves. Thus, they achieved the epitome in idolatry. And we, who are their descendants and live in the post-fall era, continue that flight from God, always claiming that we, like our first parents, have no need of God.

However, in spite of human sin and humanity's rejection of him, God would not be thwarted by a mere created being. Thus, he called Israel to bear witness to his intent to dwell with his people, and he finally fulfilled that intention in the incarnation when he entered this world as a baby in the manger in Bethlehem. Whether humankind had sinned or not, Jesus would have come, for he was the precise reason that God created humankind in the first place. He created them that they might have precisely this relation with him. Therefore, had we never sinned, the incarnation would have been the culmination of God's story with us. But such was not the case, for God came to a creature who denied his existence, and the most horrible form of that denial is seen in Christ's cross on Calvary.

The crucifixion of Jesus Christ is humanity's last gasp attempt to relieve themselves of God. There humanity nailed the Son of God to the cross, watched him die their human death, and rejoiced that they were now gods, rid of the God who would call them to be something different from what they wished to be. But on Easter Sunday morning, human hopes for their own divine status were shattered, for two women went to the tomb of their Lord, and discovered it empty. As Paul tells us, the risen Lord appeared to Peter, then to the twelve, then to many other followers, and then finally to Paul himself. In the resurrection God shows us the lie of our existence, for he tells us that his eternal purpose to be with us will never be thwarted, no matter how badly we want to rid ourselves of him. He will stand with us, sinners that we are, and he will never leave us to our own devices. He is a God of love, who will not permit his beloved children to be ultimately separated from him. Thus, in the incarnation we see God's eternal purpose for his people to be with him. In the cross we see the final human act of rejection of God, and the Son's incredible willingness to stand with us so totally that he would even die the death we deserved and suffer the separation from his Father that was rightly ours. Finally, we see in the resurrection God's affirmation of his eternal purpose, worked out in the inner-trinitarian decree, to stand always and finally with his creature.

Human Destiny

What then does all this say about the ultimate destiny of humanity? First, it affirms that we do not wait for fellowship with God, but rather we already have it, even though we often do not realize or sense God's presence with us. He is with us in Jesus Christ as Jesus Christ is made present to us by the Holy Spirit. This gives us the assurance that our relationship with Christ can never be broken in this life, and will never be broken in the next. Eternal life has begun in the present moment.

Secondly, as we look at our resurrected Lord, we discover something of what our own resurrected life will be like. We learn that there is continuity between this body we now bear and the resurrected body that we will ultimately have. The entire doctrine of resurrection as understood within a Hebraic context says that the body is good, is God-created, and that human beings will stand before their God as identifiable persons, complete with a resurrected body. We do not shed the body as if it were something evil to be lost and left behind, but rather we receive it back in its most perfected form when we enter God's presence. The body is part of our identity. But for all the continuity, there is also discontinuity, for we see in Jesus' own resurrection body a difference from his earthly body. His resurrection body could appear and disappear, it could pass through walls and doors, and yet, it was tangible, touchable, and visible. The Reformed tradition also reads I Cor. 15:35 ff., but reads it differently than do Mormons. Reformed Christians hold that in its total context the passage is simply comparing the earthly body with the resurrection body, and using various examples to stress the difference in glory between the two. The passage does not speak, in the exegesis of the Reformed tradition, of differing types of resurrection bodies, but only of the difference between one's earthly body and one's resurrected being. Beyond this, the Bible is essentially silent on life beyond death. Thus, so are theologians of the Reformed tradition. We affirm that God already dwells with us, and thus we can expect to dwell with him after our deaths. We can affirm that there is continuity between our physical being now and our resurrected being in the future, and that there is a significant degree of difference between the plainness of the one and the glory of the other. But beyond this we dare not go, for scripture does not lead us further.

Freedom of the Will

If one stresses God's eternal intent to be gracious toward his creature, what then happens to human freedom? If one argues that Christ's atoning death is all encompassing, is there any room left for human decision? Here the answer has to be both a yes and a no. If Christ's atoning death is effective for all—regardless of knowledge, actions, or decisions—then it is God, and not his creatures, who determines the *eternal* destiny of every person. His determination in the inner-trinitarian decree was to dwell with humanity as a human. He determined to dwell even with *sinful* humanity, and fulfilled that intent in the life, death, and resurrection of Jesus Christ. Thus, God has *always* chosen human beings as his own, and he will never let them go. Therefore, in terms of our ultimate end, all persons are predestined by God for fellowship with himself in and through Jesus Christ. In terms of eternal life, God has made all necessary decisions based on his love for us in Jesus Christ, and we can not finally resist that love.

HOWEVER, in terms of a *temporal* response, people either have *no* ability to choose for good or they have *total* freedom of the will. For the person whom God's Spirit has not yet touched and who has not yet received the gift of faith, there is no freedom. There is only sin. There is only flight from God. There is no desire to turn back. That person flies in a headlong rush toward self-destruction. There is no direction to life, no hope for the future. All is dark, dismal, and without purpose. Such a person has no power to choose any other existence. He or she is imprisoned in a darkened cell with no visible windows or doors.

But suddenly, a miracle occurs. The Spirit of Jesus Christ rests on that imprisoned individual, opens the eyes, unstops the ears, and turns on the lights. In an instant, one sees the key in the door, the stairway to freedom, and the blue sky beyond. *Now* one has freedom. The person can either choose freely to run to the light or to turn from it, deny its reality, and struggle against it. Yet, like the Pied Piper of Hamlin, Christ's Spirit will summon us to follow him. Some days we will use our freedom to obey and walk toward the light of day, and at other times, we will let our fears overcome us, convincing us that we see only an illusion. Christian freedom means that we constantly struggle against ourselves. We, like Paul, cry out, "Who will deliver me from this body of death? Thanks be to God through Jesus Christ our Lord!" (Rom. 7:25). That cry is possible only for the Christian who has been *given* his or her freedom by Christ. It is not the cry of the person who has never experienced God's presence. It is not the cry of a person who stands daily at some supposed cross-roads of good and evil—for no one ever stands in that position. Rather, Christ meets us on the path to self-destruction, and grants us the freedom through the gift of faith to follow him. Is there freedom of the will? Absolutely, for it is precisely this that Christ's life-giving Spirit gives to his disciples.

Hell?

One last question remains to be answered, if we follow the thesis that the incarnation is central to God's inner-trinitarian purposes. That is the question, "What happened to hell?" For those who have followed the argument thus far, they will have come to the realization that the possibility is very present for a doctrine of universal salvation, based upon Christ's all encompassing act in the incarnation and at the cross. If God's intent were to dwell with all human beings, even sinful human beings, and if Christ so utterly identified with all humanity at the cross that he actually stood in their stead for their sins, then what remains for which anyone may be damned? As we consider this issue, we should make clear that we are really asking the question whether anything final and definitive happened in the cross of Jesus Christ, or whether there is something we must do to complete his act. Traditional evangelical theology has said that the act is complete, *if* we accept it. In other words, God offers us a salvation which he has worked out on the cross of Christ, but we must accept that offer through our free will. In essence, we must complete the incomplete act of God. We must have faith. But in those terms, faith becomes an exalted human work. Even if one claims that the faith is a gift of God, then one is still faced with the problem that God seems to give faith to some and not to others, and if faith is the touchstone upon which salvation ultimately turns, God intentionally damns some persons to whom he does not give faith. Both of these positions are at variance with what we see in Jesus Christ, which is God with humankind—one man damned on behalf of all people, and one man exalted in whom all humanity is caught up.

In considering the extent of God's grace, it might be helpful to visualize a football field. The left side line runs along the edge of a cliff. One team snaps the ball and the quarterback fades back to pass. He shoots that pass into the left flat, but it is slightly overthrown. If one were the split-end on that side of the field, it is doubtful that he would run too fast to try to reach the ball, knowing that his headlong rush might drive him over the cliff and to destruction. However, if someone builds a substantial fence along the edge of the field, then the opportunity for the split-end to get to the ball is greatly enhanced. He may run into the

97

fence, but he certainly will not go over the cliff. Such is the nature of Christ's cross—it is God's fence around our playing field. If we know of the presence of that fence, then we can play the game of life fully and completely. However, if we are unaware that a fence is there, then we still live our lives in the fear that we will fall over the cliff, if we get too close to it. The fact that we do not know the fence is there, certainly does not deny the fence and its reality. It simply denies the fact that we derive any emotional benefit from it. However, those persons who know the fence is there and have discovered the joys of playing the game with freedom, should have the graciousness to inform those who do not know of its presence that it is there, so that they too may participate in the freedom the fence gives. It will be good news to them that they no longer need to live in fear.

Returning to the reality of the cross, Christians know that God has placed an impregnable barrier between all humanity and the perils of hell. They know that they worship God out of thanksgiving and rejoicing, and not out of a fear that if they don't believe, they may end up in hell. Therefore, they proclaim *good news* to their neighbors who are unaware of the magnitude and the graciousness of their God who had chosen them as his partners from all eternity. Those persons who will not accept the fact that there is a fence surrounding the field will continue to live their lives in a state of terror and panic. But upon their deaths, they will learn what they have missed and how pointless their lives were. That is sad, but that ignorance is not eternally damning, for their salvation never did depend upon their knowledge of the existence of the fence or the cross. Rather it was dependent solely upon God's own finished and complete act which took place in the incarnation, the death, and the resurrection of Jesus Christ. We proclaim the good news of the gospel, so that people may live in joy and freedom before their God. We proclaim the good news of Jesus Christ, so that all persons may begin to experience the joys of eternal life now.

And so, what has become of hell? Jesus Christ has slammed the door shut and nailed it tight for all eternity. For some, hell seems to be a necessary place for those persons with whom they do not wish to spend eternity. Thank heaven that in his inner-trinitarian decree, God was far more gracious than the creatures whom he created. In Jesus Christ we see that God stands with us eternally, and that he will never, ever, let us go.

Reflections

Plan

As we consider the material of this chapter, it would be helpful to refer to the chart (p. 102) which displays three perspectives on salvation history. The perspectives represent (1) the thought of most traditional theologians within the Church, (2) the position of the Mormon church, and (3) the position of some neo-orthodox theologians, most notably Karl Barth. The first thing we should note as we view the chart is that the basic events of salvation history are present in all, but there are differences in what is *stressed*. For example, the more traditional view of salvation history sees the cross as the central event, whereas the neo-orthodox position is incarnational in its focus, and thus Christmas becomes the central point. Because of its stress on the *process* of eternal progression, it is difficult to pick out a central point in Mormon salvation history, but all the basic elements are present within it. There are certainly differences evidenced in the histories of salvation. The variations in the concepts of the Trinity are noted by the differences in the drawings. The stick figure in the L.D.S. sequence represents the Father as a corporeal being. Also, it has been noted that there is a belief in a pre-existence among L.D.S. There is also a difference in whether humanity, mortality, free choice, and the ability to procreate precede or follow the fall. In Mormon thought there are two witnesses to Jesus Christ—the Israel-ites and the Nephites—where only the Israelites are present in traditional and neo-orthodox views. In all of the traditions the incarnation, the death, and the resurrection of Jesus Christ are evident.

Some differences in the traditions also appear when one considers the after-life. In the traditional salvation history, those who accept Christ enter into God's presence, while those who do not are viewed as damned. Thus, a great many people fall short of the glory of God and pass out of his presence. In Mormon thought the majority of human beings, because of Christ's atonement, are permitted to enter some degree of glory, but only those who have fulfilled all the commandments and ordinances of God may enter into the highest degree of glory. Hell actually contains a very few persons following the second resurrection. In the neo-orthodox tradition God's approach to humanity and Christ's death for all persons leaves no room for a concept of hell. Consequently all persons enter into the presence of God, not because of their own merits or because of anything that they have done, but solely because of God's election of them in Jesus Christ from all eternity.

There can be no question that all three of these tradi-tions deal with the God of the scriptures and with Jesus Christ as the manifestation of God, in whatever way one may actually understand that manifestation. Further, there can be no doubt that all three of the traditions seek to explain the mystery of God's grace in relationship to his creatures. True, there are exegetical differences between them which lead to differences in detail. But those differences are not significant enough to thwart the ability of Christians to kneel before their common God in worship, prayer, and praise.

It is also very clear that in all three of the histories there is a very clear plan of God rooted in eternity. In the Mormon tradition, God the Father announces the plan of salvation in the pre-existence to his spirit children who sanction and accept it. In the inner-trinitarian decree of the neo-orthodox tradition, God elects *all* humanity in Jesus Christ, and thus all of his successive acts beginning with creation and culminating in the incarnation, death, and resurrection of Jesus Christ are the fulfillment and completion of that election and decree. In the more traditional view of salvation history God has foreknowledge which sees that man will sin, thereby necessitating the salvific act in Jesus Christ. Thus, God in his foreknowledge plans to send Christ as Savior from eternity thereby freeing those who believe in his atoning death.

Grace

This entire chapter has dealt chiefly with the goodness and graciousness of God as manifest in his plan for the salvation of his people. Thus, it is fitting that we ask what grace is. For the traditionalist, grace is God's willingness to place his Son's life on the line for us, thereby freeing us from sin. For the Mormon, grace can be understood as the Father's desire to see that his children all have the same opportunity to progress and attain the exaltation that he did, and therefore he provided a plan and a path whereby they might achieve this end. And for the neo-orthodox tradition, grace can only be seen as God's giving of himself as a creature to and for his creature out of love, but not out of necessity. In each tradition, people respond to that *grace*. Mormons and traditionalists hold that our response to grace will determine the eternal destiny of each individual. On the other hand, I have argued that the way we respond determines the quality of our temporal existence, but that God has fixed our eternal destinies.

In the final analysis there are differences between these various traditions. But the *similarities* between them far overshadow any differences that may exist. Perhaps we of the Reformed and the Mormon traditions would do well to celebrate those major points of commonality, and sit quietly with one another as we seek a deeper understanding of the God who has come to us in Jesus Christ, and who has set us all free.

PERSPECTIVES ON SALVATION HISTORY

TRADITIONAL: Eternal Purpose out of God's Foreknowledge of our Sin is *to save* to Eternal Life.

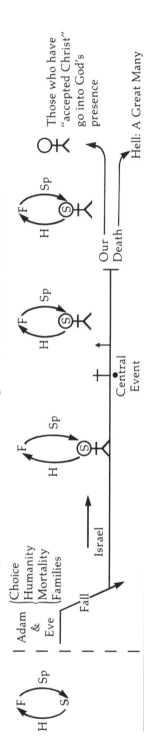

Those who have "accepted Christ" go into God's presence

Hell: A Great Many

L.D.S.: God's Eternal Purpose is to Bring Immortality and Eternal Life to Man (Moses 1:39) through Christ's Atonement.

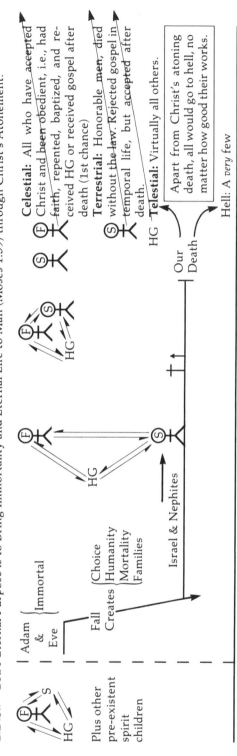

Celestial: All who have accepted Christ and been obedient, i.e., had faith, repented, baptized, and received HG or received gospel after death (1st chance)

Terrestrial: Honorable men, died without the law. Rejected gospel in temporal life, but accepted after death.

Telestial: Virtually all others.

Apart from Christ's atoning death, all would go to hell, no matter how good their works.

Hell: A *very few*

SOME NEO-ORTHODOX: Eternal Purpose of God to Be with Us (Emmanuel) as *Man* for All Eternity.

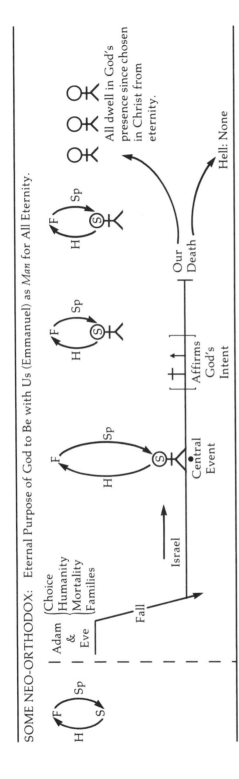

"[Teach] Them To 8
Observe All That I
Have Commanded You"
Matthew 28:20

Mormons: Faith and Works
"By their fruits shall ye know them"

Salvation/Exaltation

As we begin to deal with works in Mormon theology, we must glance behind us. We have already noted that Christ's atoning death opens the door to any of the three heavens—the celestial, the terrestrial, and the telestial—by granting all immortality and freedom from both temporal and spiritual death. Christ's atonement removes the curse of Adam's sin, and enables all persons to be accountable for their own actions. It also ultimately removes the separation from God, which is spiritual death, by enabling almost all persons to reside in the presence of some member of the Godhead. Even those who ultimately occupy the telestial kingdom will enjoy the presence of the Holy Ghost, and thus of God in a derivative way. We have further noted that there are gradations within each of the levels of heaven, and these gradations are based upon the growth in knowledge and spiritual maturity evidenced in individuals.

Beyond the general immortality wrought by Christ's atoning death, there is also a conditional salvation, or more properly a state of exaltation, which is based upon accepting and fulfilling God's plan of salvation. The required steps in

105

this plan are: (1) faith in the Lord Jesus Christ; (2) repentance; (3) baptism by immersion by someone having the authority of the priesthood; (4) the laying on of hands for the gift of the Holy Ghost by someone holding the Melchizedek Priesthood; and (5) living from that point on a righteous life in congruence with the commands of God.

The degree to which persons gain knowledge and act righteously during their mortal existence determines the level of progression they will initially achieve in any one of the three heavens. However, obedient Mormons seek to be as much like their Lord Jesus Christ as they can be, and they take seriously his command to be perfect like their Father in heaven. Consequently, they seek to live moral and upright lives in accordance with the commandments that God has given to all Mormon Christians through the priesthood and through the scriptures. Access to exaltation, or to the highest level of the celestial heaven, is gained through the doorway of celestial marriage. We have already seen that the family unit is central to Mormon faith and life, and the fundamental reason is that it opens the highest of all heavens to the believer, for one cannot be fully exalted as a single person. Male and female were meant to live together and to be sealed to one another for time and eternity. A husband and wife who gain full exaltation will have not just immortality but eternal life—life like God the Father has. They will have spirit children in their resurrected life, and they will stand in relationship to them in precisely the same way the Father God stands in relationship to us. Then, in that sense, they shall be gods because they will have no end, they will have gained authority and power like their Father God and like the power and authority of Jesus Christ. For them salvation will mean glory, authority, majesty, power, and dominion, just as it means that for their exalted Lord, Jesus Christ. Thus, while Jesus Christ's atoning death opens immortality to virtually all, a righteous life, lived in accordance with God's command and under the guidance of God's eternal priesthood, opens the door to eternal life, to total and complete salvation, or to exaltation. In this sense the works of an individual do matter and do distinguish one person from another in glory. Therefore, Joseph Fielding Smith can write the following:

> Full salvation is attained by virtue of knowledge, truth, righteousness, and all true principles. Many conditions must exist in order to make such salvation available to men. Without the atonement, the gospel, the priesthood, and the sealing power, there would be no salvation. Without continuous revelation, the ministering of angels, the working of miracles, the prevalence of gifts of the spirit, there would be no salvation. If it had not been for Joseph Smith and the restoration, there would be no salvation. There is no salvation outside The Church of Jesus Christ of Latter-day Saints (*Doctrines*, Vol. 2, pp. 1–350).

We have to realize that the Mormons are using the word salvation here in a way slightly different from that in which it is used in Catholic or Protestant circles. In Catholic/Protestant theology salvation generally means escaping the tentacles of hell, and thereby entering into the presence of God by virtue of Christ's atoning death. In Mormon thought, Christ's atoning death guarantees resurrection and immortality and a place in one of the three heavens for most people, but not necessarily "full salvation" in Mormon terminology. Salvation, which is another word for exaltation, is that toward which all persons are called to move by God's eternal plan. The plan of salvation was put into motion in order that the Father's spirit children all might become as he, if they kept their mortal estate, and if they gained knowledge and learned to choose between good and evil. Wherever the priesthood was present in human history, there also the plan of salvation was known, for the priesthood was the power of God. Wherever the priesthood was not present, the knowledge of God's plan of salvation was therefore also not wholly present, and thus salvation or exaltation was not available to anyone. Hence, Joseph Fielding Smith's statement that but for the restoration through Joseph Smith there would be no salvation. In Mormon belief, the priesthood had ceased to be present until it was restored to the earth when Peter, James, and John laid their hands on Joseph Smith and conferred the Melchizedek priesthood upon him. At that time, the fuller knowledge of God's plan of salvation once again became present upon earth, and one can say, if one holds the Mormon position, that apart from Joseph Smith salvation in the sense of full exaltation would not have been available and accessible to modern people. The logical extension of this thought is that apart from the one place where the priesthood exists, i.e., the Mormon church, there is no salvation as defined above. Knowledge of the plan requires the *proper* mediating agency and authority, and in Mormon belief that exists only within The Church of Jesus Christ of Latter-day Saints. Fundamentally, God is very gracious to all of his creatures, but he does not abrogate the free will of any of them. While he in essence condemns very few, and provides immortality and glorious resurrected lives to virtually all, he summons those who are of the purest and most perfected natures to a level of existence that transcends the majority. He summons them to exaltation or to salvation, and he summons them to work out their own salvation on the basis of their obedience and of their works.

Obedience

For the above reasons, Mormons take very seriously the law of God. It is not a burden to them, anymore than it was for the Old Testament Jew. The law of God is given that they might be safe and know his will for them on a daily basis. They rejoice in God's commandments and in God's law. It should not be a stick with which God beats them over the head, anymore than it was for the Jew. It is a manifestation of God's graciousness and of his concern for his creature. In Mormon thought, it can also serve as a test, since one of the opportunities that mortal existence provides is the opportunity to choose between good and evil, between God's law and the world's law.

Perhaps the most visible manifestation of God's law and the one which marks the Mormons as a peculiar people, is what is known as the Word of Wisdom. This is a revelation, recorded in section 89 of the Doctrine and Covenants, which came to Joseph Smith on February 27, 1833. In it he and his followers are commanded to use no alcoholic beverages, tobacco, or hot drinks, and it goes on to give various suggestions about proper diet. In modern terminology, this generally means to non-Mormons that Mormons may not smoke, drink alcoholic beverages, coffee, or tea. Adherence to the Word of Wisdom provides a discipline in Mormon lives that then permeates all other aspects of life. It helps them to be disciplined individuals and to stand up for what they believe. If Mormons can abide by the Word of Wisdom, they also gain the discipline to abide by the many other commands of God, which ultimately lead them to exaltation. The path of eternal progression has been opened wide through Jesus Christ, and all are called to place their feet upon it, as they come to know the fullness of God's plan through his authoritative Melchizedek priesthood.

The Temple and its Ordinances

To persons who are not Mormons, the temples of the Mormon church have always held a certain fascination, especially since non-Mormons are not permitted to enter them once the temple has been dedicated. Just as the temple in ancient Israel was a particularly holy place for the Jewish people, and certain portions of it were so holy that only the high priest could enter it one time each year on behalf of the people, so also the temples of The Church of Jesus Christ of Latter-day Saints are especially holy places to the members of that church. Only persons who have led morally upright and exemplary lives are permitted to enter the temple. Only those who have exhibited a deep faith in Christ and spiritual maturity may go there. As Mormons so often say, the temple is not a secret place but rather a sacred place, and thus any who would not recognize it as such are excluded. Many non-Mormons are offended that they may not enter the temple, but this is not a justifiable reaction. The non-Mormon would enter the temple out of curiosity, while the Mormon enters it out of reverence for and devotion to his or her God. What the non-Mormon would perceive as strange rituals and meaningless actions, the Mormon perceives as uplifting pointers to his or her God. In the Mormon mind, that which comes from above is sacred, and must be spoken of and experienced with constraint, solemnity, and faith. Thus, limitations are placed on temple attendance.

To enter the temple Mormons must receive temple recommends from their bishop annually. To gain the recommend persons respond to the following questions:

1. Do you believe in God the Eternal Father, in his Son Jesus Christ, and in the Holy Ghost; and do you have a firm testimony of the restored gospel?
2. Do you sustain the President of The Church of Jesus Christ of Latter-day Saints as the Prophet, Seer, and Revelator; and do you recognize him as the only person on the earth authorized to exercise all priesthood keys?
3. Do you sustain the other General Authorities and the local authorities of the Church?
4. Is there anything in your conduct relating to members of your family that is not in harmony with the teachings of the Church?
5. Do you affiliate with any group or individual whose teachings or practices are contrary to or oppose those accepted by The Church of Jesus Christ of Latter-day Saints, or do you sympathize with the precepts of any such group or individual?
6. Do you earnestly strive to do your duty in the Church, to attend your sacrament, priesthood, and other meetings; and to obey the rules, laws, and commandments of the gospel?
7. Are you a full tithe payer?

8. Do you keep the Word of Wisdom?
9. Have you ever had a divorce that has not been cleared by appropriate priesthood authorities where required?
10. If you have ever been divorced or separated, are you presently fulfilling your obligations for the support and maintenance of your family?
11. If you have received your temple endowment—
    a. Do you keep all the covenants that you made in the temple?
    b. Do you wear the authorized garments both day and night?
12. Do you live the law of chastity?
13. Has there been any sin or misdeed in your life that should have been resolved with priesthood authorities but has not?
14. Do you consider yourself worthy in every way to enter the temple and participate in temple ordinances?

All the questions are self-explanatory, and seek to lead the church member to the heights of Christian ethics and morality. The only question that might seem strange to Christians who are not Mormons is question number five. It is asked primarily to identify persons who may still advocate or practice polygamy as an authorized doctrine of the church. Polygamy has been banned by the church, and thus to practice it would be at variance with the commands and counsels of the priesthood. The quality of moral life that is expected of temple-going Mormons is such that perhaps all should wish that their neighbors were Mormons who went to the temple regularly.

Clearly, the temple is a very special place. To date the Mormons have constructed twenty-eight temples, the one at Nauvoo having been destroyed by fire in the early history of the church. They also have a number of new temples under construction and on the drawing board.

Three basic ordinances occur in Mormon temples. First, is the giving of the endowment. Secondly, sealings are accomplished for both the living and the dead. And finally, baptism is performed on behalf of dead ancestors.

Endowment

The first experience that people have with the temple is the receiving of the endowment. Fundamentally, it is a process through which individuals hear about and see enacted God's plan of salvation. They hear once again the story of their pre-existence, God's purpose in the creation of the world, the reason for Christ's coming, the falling away of the authority in Christ's Church, and finally the restoration of the Church through Joseph Smith. In the experience of the endowment, persons also receive certain promises and make certain promises of a spiritual nature which will sustain and carry them through life. The garment which all Mormons who have been to the temple wear next to their bodies is a reminder of their temple experience. There are certain marks on the garment itself that are designed to call the Mormon's attention regularly to the promises and covenants that were made in the temple before their God. It is a misconception on the part of non-Mormons or even of Mormons to suppose that somehow the garment is a magical amulet that protects them from all harm. It does so only in the sense that as they keep the covenants made before their God, they will remain safe spiritually. The garment is an ever-present reminder of God's plan and of God's call to individual holiness in and through Christ.

There is one portion of the endowment drama that deserves a special note, for it portrays a discussion between Adam, Lucifer, and a Preacher. Many non-Mormons find this segment particularly offensive, but is the offense justified? Granted, the Preacher is portrayed as college trained, a seminary graduate, and a sophisticate in things theological, but he is also a servant of Lucifer. His job is to preach "right *religion*" to Adam and his offspring. If he does so and converts them to this "right religion," Lucifer will pay him well. But the real issue is not the Preacher. Rather, it is the conflict between "right *religion*" and "right *relationships.*" A very short quote from a section of the conversation between these three personages is in order here:

> Lucifer: Do you preach orthodox religion?
> Preacher: Yes, that is what I preach.
> Lucifer: Well, if you'll preach your orthodox religion to this people and convert them, I'll pay you well.
> Preacher: I'll do my best. Good morning, sir.
> Adam: Good morning.
> Preacher: I understand you are looking for *religion* (italics mine).
> Adam: I was calling upon *Father.*

(From a pamphlet published by Ex-Mormons for Jesus, Phoenix, Arizona.)

Clearly, there is some polemic against paid ministry and "orthodoxy," and little wonder. The doctrine of the restoration of the authority of Christ's Church clearly questions what has gone before it. This should not be surprising or new to the readers of this book. However, to end our consideration of this scene with that thought is to fail to understand its deeper significance.

We should note that the antithesis is not between Mormons and non-Mormons, but rather between *religion* and seeking *Father.* It is a contrast between adherence to a set of unquestioned *doctrines* (the Preacher) and the personal relationship between an individual (Adam) and God. This drama is a *warning* to *Mormons* not to lose the relationship between themselves and God by supplanting it with sterile, undigested, and unexamined dogmas. *Both* Mormons and non-Mormons need to hear and heed this warning. Every human being is guilty of substituting *things* (particularly doctrines) for a vital, living relationship with God. If this were not so, there would be no religious controversy. If *Mormons* simply go through the motions of religious life and

113

claim to have found "religion," they stand condemned themselves, and become the "preacher" in the drama. So also *non-Mormons* are rightly condemned by the drama who argue that if persons don't believe the same doctrines, do the same acts, and live the same lives as the "preacher," they can't possibly be accepted by the Father. If we, Mormons and non-Mormons, look in the mirror of this little drama and see ourselves, we should stop and think about the real essence of Christianity—i.e., faith which creates a relationship with God through Jesus Christ, and not through sterile rules, laws, or the doctrines of *anyone*.

Celestial Marriage

As noted earlier, the door to exaltation is opened through the ordinance of celestial marriage. This is marriage performed by a person who holds the authority to bind two people together not only for this temporal life but also for all eternity. The family is the central unit within Mormonism, and as a family they are sealed together with the hope and expectation that they will attain exaltation through their obedience to God's precepts and to God's commands. In obedience, they will want to be sealed for time and eternity, and become perfect as their Father in heaven is perfect. Thus, the act of sealing persons in marriage is one of the central reasons for the existence of temples in the Mormon church. Therefore, a young Mormon couple goes to the temple to be sealed, rather than having a public marriage ceremony as do Protestants or Catholics. For families who have a son or daughter who has converted to Mormonism and then been married in the temple, this can be a very difficult time for they, as non-Mormons, will not be able to be present at the marriage and sealing. The Church of Jesus Christ of Latter-day Saints has taken some steps, however, to ease the disappointment for non-member parents or even for member parents who do not have temple recommends. In some temples, there are special family rooms where parents may be with their children prior to the sealing, where the significance of what is being done for the children can be explained to parents by the sealer, and to which the couple may return immediately following the sealing. While such acts do not remove the desire of parents to be present at the sealing of their children, they do demonstrate a commitment on the part of the Mormon church to keep the family unit bound together, while at the same time adhering to the sacred character of the temple.

Perhaps this discussion of the role and function of the temple in Mormon life will give to non-member parents a better understanding and appreciation of the importance of celestial marriage in the lives of their converted children.

Sealing of Families

In the event that a couple is married who already has children from previous marriages, these children will be sealed to their new parents, if they were not sealed to prior parents as might have been the case if one parent were to have died. Sealings in the temple may be broken in the event of a divorce, but because the sealing was done for time and eternity by one having the authority to bind on earth as well as heaven, such a breaking of the sealing requires the official act of the living prophet. He is the only earthly individual who has the authority to break what is not only sealed on earth but also sealed in heaven. Few temple marriages end in divorce. This says a great deal about the seriousness with which Mormons take their temple vows.

Baptism and Sealing for Dead Ancestors

Since Mormons believe that persons who did not have the opportunity to hear the restored gospel proclaimed in this life will have the opportunity to hear it in the next, they are expected to perform certain external ordinances on behalf of dead ancestors. This vicarious work is rooted in Jesus' own vicarious work on our behalf. If Jesus could die an atoning death for us, then we also can carry out vicarious

115

acts, by God's permission, on behalf of others. Mormons do extensive genealogical work in order to identify ancestors. When the gospel is preached to them in the next life and if they accept it, temple work will need to be done for them, since they would be unable to fulfill all ordinances on their side of the veil. Thus, there are certain ordinances which God requires living persons to carry out on behalf of their deceased ancestors in the temple. Baptism and sealing for the dead are these ordinances.

Mormons believe that one must, after having reached the age of accountability (8 years) be baptized by immersion in water. However, water is an element of a physical nature and not of a heavenly one. Water is not available to persons who may hear and accept the gospel in the next life, and if they are to proceed on the path of eternal progression, they must fulfill the plan of salvation. They must have faith in Jesus Christ, repent, be *baptized* by immersion, receive the Holy Ghost through the laying on of hands, and keep all of the commandments of God. All but the water baptism may be accomplished in the next life. Thus, in the event the ancestors hear the gospel and accept it, the necessary act of immersion in water will have been performed in the temple on their behalf. The necessity of this water baptism is rooted in Jesus himself, who, though he had no sin, was required by the Father, according to Mormon thought, to experience water baptism. In like manner, vicarious sealing for dead ancestors is necessary. Provided the deceased ancestors receive Christ in the next world, sealing on their behalf opens the celestial kingdom and exaltation to them just as surely as if they had done it themselves.

Some persons, who are not Mormon, find baptisms for the dead to be highly pretentious, but a Mormon understands them to be acts of love in which the family is bound together. (See I Cor 15:29.) The right to accept or not accept the gospel as it is proclaimed in the next life rests with individuals, but if one believes as the Mormons do, it would be an incredibly callous act not to fulfill God's plan by carrying out the obligation to do the genealogical work and to be baptized and sealed for one's dead ancestors.

The temple—sacred but not secret. It is a place that is holy to those who perceive it as such. It is a place where all dress alike in white and stand before their God in complete equality. It is the place where millionaire and pauper, king and commoner, apostle and church member, all can stand before their God in humility and reverence, and wait for that still small voice to speak to them. It is the place where they hear the gospel proclaimed in a very graphic way. It is the place of peace, of solitude, of joy, and of fulfillment. It is a house where Christ is the beginning and the end and where the pure in heart may truly commune with him.

Finally, to those who would argue that the temple ritual is "warmed over Masonry," it would have to be said that they neither understand the Masons nor the Mormons. Masonry is fundamentally *fraternal*. It binds people to people. The temple rites, whatever their origin, are wholly Christological, binding people to the God whom they have met in Jesus Christ. To Mormons the temple is a sacred place, and should be respected as such by all.

The Sacrament

A very important part of Mormon spiritual growth is to be found in the sacrament—i.e., the Lord's Supper. Its regular celebration in weekly Sacrament Meeting on Sunday is rooted in the New Testament (Matt. 26:26–29; Mark 14:22–25; Luke 22:15–20), the Book of Mormon (Mosiah 18:7–10; 3 Ne. 18) and the Doctrine and Covenants (84:44; 20:75). The sacrament is to be taken by worthy persons and calls individuals to remember Christ's body and blood which were given for the sins of the world, to take upon themselves Christ's name, and to keep God's commandments. To those who partake of the sacrament worthily, God gives his guiding Spirit and the promise that the person shall inherit eternal life. Each week there is a recommitment and a rededication of members of the Mormon church in Sacrament Meeting.

The Reformed Tradition: Faith and Works
"Faith without works is dead"

Faith

Among Reformed Christians, as noted above, Christ's once-for-all atoning death and his subsequent resurrection affirm God's eternal intent to dwell with his children as a person. God will not permit his children to drive an ultimate and eternal wedge between creature and creator, and thus out of his love and graciousness God not only comes to us, but bridges the gap that we created between ourselves and God. The reconciliation of God and humanity is finished and perfect in Jesus Christ. That is the objective side of the coin. However, God's intent is to dwell with his creatures in this world and for those creatures to be *aware* of his presence and his act on their behalf. In order that humanity may rejoice in the presence of their God, Christ provides his people with one more thing—faith. Faith is God's gift to the members of his Church, a gift through which those members appropriate in an experiential way the joy and the power of their daily walk with God.

A critical verse for understanding the role of faith, over against God's reconciling act in Jesus Christ for all humanity, is Rom. 5:1. The verse says, "Therefore, having been put right with God through faith we have peace with God through our Lord Jesus Christ." In the Greek there is no punctuation in this sentence, and thus the question is raised whether we are *put right* with God through faith, or whether through faith we have *peace* with our God? In our earlier discussion of Christ's act on our behalf and in fulfillment of the inner-trinitarian decree, we rejected the idea that faith is something that humankind must *add* to Christ's act to make it complete. Therefore, when we consider this sentence in

Rom. 5:1, we cannot punctuate it, as Christendom has so often done, as "Therefore, having been *put right* with God *through faith*, we have peace with God through our Lord Jesus Christ." Rather, the punctuation should be, "Therefore, having been put right with God, *through faith* we *have peace* with God through our Lord Jesus Christ." Faith is not a human act which caps God's almost complete act on our behalf at the cross. Instead, faith is God's gift to those persons whom he chooses to be his witnesses within the world, and faith is the human experience of living in relationship with God. Faith is the Christian's joyful and obedient response to the God who has already come to humanity and made all things new, even while human beings are still in sinful flight from him.

Law

God does not, however, leave his people to wonder what the proper response is to him, and how they may live life safely in his presence. Like any loving father, God places a fence around his children to keep them from harm, and theologically this fence consists of his law.

Within Christendom there has been a great deal of discussion about the role and function of the law in Christian life. In broad terms, Luther held that the law was given by God to highlight the fact that apart from God's reconciling and justifying act in Jesus Christ, there was no hope for a person to attain righteousness before God. The law served to show individuals how far short of righteousness they actually fell. Apart from faith in Jesus Christ, there could be no hope of human justification before God. Essentially, desperation before humanity's inability to keep the law would drive people joyfully to the gospel and to faith in Jesus Christ. In Luther's thought, the demands of the law were banished by the gospel.

Calvin, however, while essentially agreeing that the law led to the gospel, still saw a role for law in the Christian

Church. He noted that while Paul continually talked about the gospel of Jesus Christ, he also ended his letters with moral and ethical directions to his people, or, in a word, with the law. For Calvin, God's law, particularly the Ten Commandments, served as a tutor and as a guide to Christians. While people were not saved by keeping the law, since that occurred in Jesus Christ, they were still *guided* by the law in their daily lives. The law was an extension of God's graciousness.

Calvin's position is very much in tune with the biblical witness, but the biblical literature even goes beyond Calvin's understanding, particularly where the Old Testament is concerned. Biblically, the law is an extension of God's grace to his people. We should note in Ex. 20:1 the statement which says, "I am the Lord your God who brought you out of the land of Egypt, out of the house of bondage. You shall have no other Gods before me" (RSV). Note that the basis for God's giving of the law is that he had acted graciously on behalf of the people *prior* to the giving of the law. God had freed his people from Egypt. He had led them through the wilderness. He had brought them to Sinai. He had chosen the people, long before they ever chose him. He had brought them to himself through his gracious acts on their behalf. At Sinai he provided them with a law, not to test them, but rather to keep them safe. Those who lived within the boundaries of the law, lived a life that could be full and complete and safe as they walked with their God. Therefore, the law was not a burden or a final exam, but rather a joy to contemplate, for it was the extension of a loving Father's graciousness.

Karl Barth wrestles with the question of the place and function of the law when he considers Romans 7 and struggles with what it means to say that the law is dead. His answer is that God's law is always God's law, and once given God does not retract it, change it, or take it away. The law which is dead is the law which human beings have created as they have taken God's gracious law and tried to turn it into a ladder by which they may clamber up to God. The law is not a stick which we hold over God demanding our rights for having kept portions of it. If we believe that the law functions in this way, then we have corrupted the law and misunderstood God's grace. But this is precisely what *all* human beings try to do with God's law. Thus, humans take God's good gift of the law, corrupt it, distort it, and substitute their human legal travesty for God's divine guidance. It is precisely this human mockery of the law that is destroyed and is dead in Jesus Christ. In his destruction of human arrogance, Christ once again frees the law to function in the way it was intended to function—i.e., as the guide to a safe life in the presence of God. Once again, law is truly an extension of God's gracious act in Jesus Christ.

Works

Clearly then, works gain no "brownie points" which God must recognize and reward. Rather they are a spontaneous product of a life lived in joy and faith before one's reconciling God. They are done out of joyful obedience to a God who has first acted on behalf of his people. Works are something that clearly distinguish men and women and the quality of their lives from one another in this life. But in Reformed theology they have absolutely no bearing upon a person's status in the next life, for God looks upon all human beings as perfect, since he sees them all in the perfection of the one perfect human being who stands in his presence—i.e., Jesus Christ. In Christ we are all perfect in the sight of God. However, in our daily lives we are all summoned by the Spirit to *become* what we already are in Jesus Christ.

Because of the Reformed Christian's recognition of God's incredible grace and the fact that as a Christian we have nothing to give back to God for which he then owes us, we experience a deep sense of responsibility for our neighbor for whom Christ has also died. If God were so incredibly gracious to us, then we, in joyful response to his act for us, can only be graciously responsible for our neighbor. Thus, there is a strong social gospel within the Reformed tradition which demands justice for all God's children in every corner of the world. One sees, therefore, Reformed Christians involved in racial issues, issues of poverty and hunger, issues of human rights, and every other issue where the human worth and dignity which God has shown to be present in his children, as he stood with them as a human being, is denied and trampled upon. Reformed Christians are called to bear the graciousness of God to all people. This is not done because they must do so to fulfill some command of God, but is done because in joy at their own salvation, they can do nothing else.

Sacraments

Baptism. Among Reformed Christians there are two sacraments—baptism and Holy Communion. Both focus on the incredible grace of God that has been made visible in Jesus Christ. Both claim Christ's actual and real presence in them. Within the Reformed tradition baptism may be done for either adults or infants. When adults respond to Christ, part of their entrance into the Church is the act of baptism. However, Reformed Christians believe that the most graphic example of God's graciousness to his people in Jesus Christ is seen in the act of *infant* baptism. Infant baptism declares graphically that God has claimed us all, long before we were ever conscious of him. In baptism we are ushered into the body of Christ, which is the Church. In baptism we are cleansed of our sins. Many would claim that infants have no sin, and therefore baptism is irrelevant to them. But is this really the case?

I once had a professor in seminary who said that he doubted the doctrine of original sin. But then he had his first child, and he began to wonder. By the time he had had his fourth, he jokingly said he believed in total depravity. But that statement is more than a joke, for in a child we see the very thing which the Genesis story claims to be the plight of all humankind—i.e., self-centeredness and the belief that we are gods. Just as Adam and Eve claimed that they were the center of the universe, and that they did not have to pay homage to anything beyond themselves, so also infants *know* that they are the center of the universe. They *know* that the world must come to a stop when they cry or when they wish to be fed. They *know* that all the world is created for the sole purpose of serving them. Thus, infant baptism declares that God accepts even the most self-centered of his creatures, long before they come to the point of confessing faith in anything outside of themselves. In the public baptism of an infant, the Church proclaims in joy that Christ walks and dwells with all of his people, even when they do not or cannot acknowledge him. We may leave God, but God never leaves us, for if he were to do so, he would deny the purpose of his inner-trinitarian decree. Baptism is the public proclamation of God's fulfillment of that decree, whether infants or adults are baptized. When infants are baptized the act of appropriating God's prior claim on them awaits the individual's mature personal response at some later time in their lives. Usually between the ages of 12 and 15, children who were baptized as infants will respond to Christ's claim on them and become professing members of his body, the Church. Thus, God's claim and human response are separated by time when an infant is baptized.

In the baptism of an adult, God's claim on that individual is still prior to any response in that person, and has been present since the moment of that individual's birth. But now, the Spirit has opened the individual's eyes to God's claim, and that person seeks to respond through a public confession of faith and the public act of baptism. Thus, chronologically, God's *claim* on the adult and that adult's response to that claim are *bound together* in the act of adult baptism. But the meaning and the content of the act of baptism does not change, whether carried out with children or adults. Christ is present and is professed as the Lord. He is the one who already claims us in his incarnation, death, and resurrection.

Holy Communion. The second sacrament, Holy Communion, also proclaims Christ's act for us, his presence with us, and the fact that our lives move toward him and his eternal kingdom. In the act of Holy Communion, the believer actually participates in the death and resurrection of Jesus Christ. One does not simply recall a past event, but as one partakes of Holy Communion one actually participates once again in Christ's death. The elements of bread and wine (or grape juice) *spiritually* become the body and the blood of our Lord which enlivens us and cleanses us of our sin. But Holy Communion is not solely a backward look, for the story of Jesus Christ does not end on the cross. Rather, he was resurrected and reigns at the right hand of God the Father for all eternity. Thus, Holy Communion is an invitation to sit down at the table of the lamb in the eschatological age, in the new Jerusalem, in the presence of God. It is an act of joy and preparation for total entry into God's kingdom. Holy Communion is, therefore, both participation in the past event of Christ's death, but also the present and future celebration of our end which is with God.

Reflections

Both Mormon Christians and Reformed Christians claim that apart from Christ's atoning death there is no salvation. There is, however, a significant difference in the way they understand the atonement to be effective. Mormons hold that Christ's atoning death provides *immortality* to all, and also a place within one of the three levels of heaven. But ultimate *salvation* or *exaltation* is conditional upon the individual's ability and desire to fulfill the plan of God. Reformed Christians, on the other hand, hold that Christ's act is utterly complete, and that its effectiveness is conditioned by nothing, except perhaps, for some theologians, by faith. Persons do not stand before God at various levels of maturity in eternity, but stand equally before God, because God sees them all through his resurrected Son. In both traditions, God is viewed as almost universally gracious, but in Mormonism some are more highly exalted and more highly rewarded than others, based upon their free choices between good and evil, between obedience and disobedience.

Some non-Mormon Christians would claim that the Christ in Mormon theology really does not save, but here we run into a difference in terminology. The non-Mormon Christian usually does not understand that Christ's atoning death is so broad that virtually all are saved from hell in the end—which is really what most non-Mormons mean by the word "salvation." The Mormon, on the other hand, means that salvation is equivalent to exaltation—i.e., to being perfect like one's Father who is in heaven and having eternal life as does he. Salvation for the Mormon means going beyond a mere escape from hell to a life of continued growth and responsibility in fellowship and companionship with one's family. The Mormon conception of salvation is pragmatic, for it incorporates the basic observation that people seem to be at different levels in their spiritual life and development. Thus, Mormons claim that there are different levels of spiritual maturity before God in heaven. The resolution of the differences between the two traditions lies in whether one understands Christ's atoning death to have simply removed the temporal and spiritual death brought about by Adam's sin, thereby opening the path of eternal progression as one gains knowledge and maturity in the faith; or whether God in his fullness really entered history and dwelt with his creature, thereby bringing all humanity into the fellowship with himself that he determined to have from all eternity. In the former, works play a role in one's eternal progression. In the latter, works are simply a response to a prior graciousness, and gain one nothing in the afterlife. All that needed to be gained has been gained in Jesus Christ.

At this juncture it would be interesting for Mormon and Reformed Christians to consider the question, "Would I be a Christian, if I did not believe in an afterlife?" Are we Christians to *get* something, or are we Christians because we have *experienced* the graciousness of God, and we simply want to walk with him? I believe it was Luther who once said that

125

to walk with him? I believe it was Luther who once said that the only person who was truly Christian was the one who would be willing to be damned to hell, if that would give glory to God. What he was saying was that true Christianity is not a religion of getting, but rather one of *giving!* Luther likened the Christian life to a man holding a large empty sack. The individual brings the sack before God, God fills it, and that person then distributes the contents to his neighbors, keeping nothing for himself. He returns to God, God fills the sack again, and the man distributes its contents once more. The Christian life is the life lived not for ourselves, but rather for others.

Dietrich Bonhoeffer in one of his writings cautioned us not to run too quickly to the New Testament with its belief in an afterlife, for he felt that many Christians have lost the vitality of the Old Testament's understanding of what it meant to live before God in *this* life. In the Old Testament, there is virtually no belief in an afterlife, except perhaps for a very late passage in Daniel (Dan. 12:2). Thus, the Jews were not obedient to their God, because they believed they would receive anything in an afterlife. Rather, they were obedient, because they had *experienced* the graciousness of their God in the leading of the Israelite people out of Egypt and out of bondage—an event in which the Jews participated annually in the Passover—and in God's giving of the law which lighted one's steps by day and by night. The Christian should be willing to walk before his or her God, whether there is an afterlife or not. The Christian is one who experiences God's goodness today, in the midst of both joy and sorrow, and knows that he or she walks with that God in every moment of life. If we cannot say this, we perhaps should ask ourselves whether we have truly heard the good news of the gospel.

Without question, there are some significant differences between the views that Reformed Christians and Mormon Christians hold of the relationship between Christ's atonement and human works. Much of the difference lies in the fact that Mormon Christians believe they see more in the

Bible about the afterlife than do Reformed Christians. Reformed Christians know that they will dwell in Christ's presence, because of God's gracious approach to them in Christ and Christ's willingness to identify totally and utterly with them not only in their life but also in their death. Mormons accept this generally, but at the same time see many biblical passages pointing them beyond mere fellowship with the divine to a life of continued growth and exaltation, with all the attendant responsibilities that accompany becoming perfect as one's Father in heaven is perfect. But even as we say this, we should ask ourselves whether doctrinal differences, based upon imperfect *human perceptions* of Jesus Christ as he is made known to us in scripture, are the basis upon which Christian fellowship is founded? Is it not far truer that Christian fellowship is to be experienced in the act of *worship* before our common God, and then only secondarily within the ivy covered walls of theological discussion and doctrinal conversations?

"If the Root is Holy, 9
So Are the Branches"
Romans 11:16

Mormons and Israel

Latter-day Israel

W. D. Davies, in his article titled "Israel, the Mormons and the Land," makes the following statement:

> "The point is that Mormons believe themselves to be Israelites in a literal sense and also to be closely related to the Indians, who are also physically descended from Israelites. The Mormons, then, are a continuation of what the fathers of the Christian Church were to come to call the Old Israel. But for Mormons there is no Old Israel. They simply regard themselves as Israel in a new state of its history" (*Reflections on Mormonism*, ed. Truman G. Madsen [Provo: BYU Religious Studies Center, 1978] p. 81.).

This is, at first glance, an astounding assertion, and yet it is true. Mormons hold that when the ten tribes were exiled in 721 B.C. by the Assyrians, the tribes eventually moved north and finally became assimilated into the broad culture of the world. Thus, humankind is permeated with the blood of Israel. All persons know that the Jews are descendants of Israel, but Mormons believe there are many other descendants who have leavened the world through intermarriage, thereby making virtually every human being a literal member of Israel. Thus, every person who becomes part of The Church of Jesus Christ of Latter-day Saints is either a descendant of Abraham by blood (the majority of persons who join the Church) or by adoption. Israel was God's true church, for Israel bore the priesthood. The Mormon church is also Israel, for nothing has changed within the priesthood. It is eternal. The only difference between Israel and the Mormon church is that Israel awaited the coming of Jesus and his atoning death, while The Church of Jesus Christ of Latter-day Saints looks back upon it as the center of time. Those few individuals in this day who are not of the literal Israelite bloodline are adopted into the lineage of Abraham (Abra. 2:9–11; *Teachings*, pp. 149–50).

Obviously with this view of their relation to Israel, there should be no anti-Semitism within Mormonism. As it says in 3 Nephi 29:8, "Yea, ye need not any longer hiss, nor spurn, nor make game of the Jews, nor any of the remnant of the house of Israel; for behold, the Lord remembereth his covenant unto them, and he will do unto them according to that which he hath sworn." Although the literal descendants of Abraham will be restored to the true church and to the fold of God as it is manifest in The Church of Jesus Christ of Latter-day Saints, it will not entail a denial of their heritage, but rather a return to the true beliefs of their forefathers. Israel will be fully restored at the time of the second coming of Christ.

The restoration of Israel will take place in two localities —in Jerusalem and in a new Jerusalem near Independence, Missouri. The house of Judah will gather in Jerusalem, and the house of Joseph will be established in America, with the ten tribes coming together on this continent (D&C 57:1–3, 110:11, 133). However, before this can occur, certain other things must first take place, and it is here that Mormon millennial thought comes into focus.

The Millennium

Mormons hold that human history will span six thousand years with an additional thousand reserved for the millennium. The nearness of the millennium (a period of peace under Christ's lordship) which will be ushered in by Christ's second coming, will be recognized by those who know how to read the signs of the times. A number of such signs Mormons believe have already occurred in the recent past and some are still occurring. The following events will herald the millennium.

1. The universal apostasy, which has already occurred between the years 100 A.D. and 1830 A.D.
2. An era of restoration, which is occurring in The Church of Jesus Christ of Latter-day Saints right now.
3. The restoration of the gospel, also occurring through the Mormon church.
4. The gospel witness to be heralded to the world, once again already occurring through the missionary activities of the Mormon church.
5. The coming forth of the Book of Mormon, which also has occurred.
6. The restoration of the kingdom to Israel, also occurring in part through the gathering of the lost ten tribes in The Church of Jesus Christ of Latter-day Saints and the renewal of Israel as a political entity.
7. The coming of Elijah, which occurred when Elijah appeared to Joseph Smith and Oliver Cowdery on April 3, 1836.
8. The sending of a messenger from before the Lord's face. This has been fulfilled in Joseph Smith and in the coming of John the Baptist.

There are still a number of signs yet to occur. Some of these are as follows.

1. Signs of the times are to be fulfilled, such as wars, rumors of wars, famine, pestilence, etc.
2. Great signs will occur in heaven and earth, such as blood, fire, and smoke.

3. Jesus will come to Adam-ondi-Ahman to receive back the keys of authority that he has given to his stewards.
4. The great battle at Armageddon will be in full swing when the Lord returns.

There are other signs that could be listed, but these suffice to give some sense of the feeling among Mormons that they live very close to the end time. It is not uncommon for Mormons to hope the millennium could arrive as early as the 21st century. Thus, past and present are rapidly converging in the Mormon faith. Scattered Israel is being gathered, Israel is being renewed, and because of that renewal the Lord's coming is rapidly approaching.

Jews and the Reformed Tradition

Anti-Semitism

The history of the mainline Christian Church with reference to their Jewish neighbors has not been a happy one. There has been a cloud of anti-Semitism that has shrouded Christian attitudes toward Jews for the last two thousand years. The world saw it take its most ghastly form in the Holocaust in Germany during the Nazi era. Those acts were defended through an Aryan Christianity which claimed to be vindicating the Lord by exterminating the descendants of those who had crucified him. Unquestionably, the anti-Semitism which excluded Jews, placed them in ghettos, slaughtered them during the inquisition, and ultimately led them to the gas ovens of Auschwitz and Bergen-Belsen, stands as a terrible judgment against the arrogance that can be fostered by exclusivistic faith.

Anti-Semitism stands as an indictment of the Christian Church generally, because there is no significant support for it in the New Testament. Both Luke and Matthew see strong continuity between Israel and the Church, not discontinuity. Matthew expresses this reality in two ways. First, in the genealogy at the beginning of his gospel, Matthew claims that Jesus is the son of David and the son of Abraham. By claiming Davidic descent for Jesus, Matthew affirms that Jesus fulfills the messianic hopes of Israel, thereby expressing continuity with Israel. His reference to Abraham is his way of affirming that Christ will be a blessing to all the nations, thereby fulfilling the Abrahamic covenant. But even more graphically, Matthew sees the whole Old Testament expectation fulfilled in Jesus, and makes this clear time after time when he uses the formula, "This was done that the scripture might be fulfilled."

In like manner, Luke also sees continuity between Israel and the Church, but since he is writing for a non-Jewish audience, and since the statement that "the scriptures have been fulfilled" would be relatively meaningless to that audience, he must resort to a different method to convey the same truth. He finds that medium in the temple and in Jerusalem. If one looks closely at the Gospel of Luke and at Acts, one sees that the significant events take place in Jerusalem and in the temple. The birth of John the Baptist is announced to his father *in the temple* in *Jerusalem*. Jesus is brought to the *temple* for circumcision. Both Simeon and Anna prophesy over the baby Jesus in *Jerusalem*. During a large portion of the Gospel of Luke, Jesus is moving inexorably toward *Jerusalem*. Jesus cleanses the *temple*, dies in *Jerusalem*, and appears to his disciples in *Jerusalem*. The disciples, following Jesus' resurrection, continue to go to and worship in the *temple*. To the gentile, who might know nothing of Jewish scripture, this stress on temple and Jerusalem made it abundantly clear that there was some connection between the Church and the Jewish traditions, for even the most untutored of gentiles might well recognize that Jerusalem and its temple were central to the faith of the Jews.

In like manner, Paul stresses the connection between the Jews and the Church, and for him this was a burning question. In Rom. 9–11, Paul wrestles with whether the persons, whom God had originally chosen to be the bearers of the promises and of his law, had fallen out of favor with

God and been replaced by another people. Were the chosen people still chosen? This is a vital issue not only for Paul, but also for us in our own day. If God could call a people and then abandon them, he could do the same with us. If the Jews, as God's chosen people, are not still his chosen people, the members of the Church can have no certainty that God has called and chosen them. They can have no certainty that God might not change his mind once more. Thus, the very trustworthiness of God is dealt with by Paul in Rom. 9–11. But Paul affirms that Israel is, indeed, still chosen. He knows that some Jewish people are already in the Church, and at least some are not cut off from it. However, he goes even further than this with the parable of the natural olive tree into which the branches of the wild olive are grafted (Rom. 11:16–32, cf. Jacob 5 – Book of Mormon). He notes with sorrow that some of the natural branches have been cut off *for a time* to permit the ingrafting of the unnatural branches —i.e., the gentiles. But even so, the roots and the stem are Israel, the Jewish descendants of Abraham. Something new has not been created, but rather something old has been continued. In the end, the fullness of Israel will be grafted back in, and Paul ends this segment with a statement that has significant universalistic overtones for both Jew and gentile. He says, "For God has made all people prisoners of disobedience, so that he might show mercy to them all" (Rom. 11:32 – RSV). Therefore, in Matthew, Luke, and Paul, one can find no reason for an anti-Semitic stance within the Church.

Unfortunately, however, the roots of anti-Semitism may lie within the New Testament itself. They may lie within a gospel that has some of the highest theological insights into the nature and being of Christ of any of the New Testament writings. This writing is the Gospel of John. In it, John uses the word "world" primarily to designate all that is opposed to God. The chief representatives of the world are, in John's view, "the Jews." By the time the Gospel of John was written, probably in the 90's, both Judaism and Christianity had begun to define themselves and the differences that existed between themselves and their sister faith. One can almost visualize the synagogue on one side of the street and the church on the other, and one can feel the animosity that by this time existed between them. It is sad that John did not convey as full a vision of the continuity between Israel and the Church as he did of the nature of our Lord, but such was not the issue with which he wrestled.

The End Time

In closing, it is appropriate to look at the relationship between Church, Israel, and the eschaton (end time). The Reformed tradition would hold that God has gathered all of his people to himself in Jesus Christ, and that he has made no distinction between Jew and Christian. Rather, the Christian is the one who believes that God entered our world in the person of Christ, and has the unique knowledge that God is triune—i.e., God is of one essence but composed of three persons. In faith the Christian appropriates that reality and lives by it, while the Jew participates in it through faith in expectation of it. The Christian knows that what the Jew still awaits has occurred. Yet, *both* participate in its reality by virtue of their faith, one participating in it in expectation with the other participating in it in retrospect.

Finally, because the Reformed tradition holds that God has already entered our world in the person of Jesus Christ, there is a tendency to de-emphasize his second coming. While we profess that God in his good pleasure will bring all things to completeness, we are not holding our breath nor are we waiting for the signs of the approaching millennium. If God entered history in Jesus Christ, then both the beginning and end of eternity have entered history, and we participate *now* in God's end time, without waiting for an additional historical act. As G. B. Caird has said in his commentary on the book of Revelation, the end is not a *time*, but rather it is a *person*—the person of Jesus Christ (G. B. Caird, *The Revelation of St. John The Divine* [New York: Harper and Row Publishers, 1966] p. 301).

Reflections

Reformed Christians have much to learn from Mormon Christians about the importance of Israel before God. The Mormons have heard the message of Matthew, Luke, and Paul with clarity. They recognize the special place that Jews hold before God. The Mormons affirm, as all must, that the chosen people are still chosen. But in their thought about themselves as true Israelites and literal descendants of Abraham, Mormons go beyond what the biblical literature itself warrants. It is not necessary to claim literal descent from Abraham, unless one holds the view of the priesthood and its eternal significance that the Mormons do. The Mormon church should hear the other side of the Matthean and Lucan message, i.e., not only did God come to the Jews, and not only is there continuity between Israel and the Church, but God also had equal concern for his people, the gentiles. Israel was a people with a *vocation*, not a status. Israel was a nation with the vocation of being a light to the world, to the gentiles, so that they might also know of God's eternal covenant to be with his people in Jesus Christ. Israel did not have an exalted position before God, but rather the privilege and vocation of proclaiming God's grace to the whole of humanity. This privilege the Jews still possess. Thus, there is a deep need for the total Church to re-examine its views on Judaism.

In light of the above discussion, Christians might do well to drop the distinctions between Old and New Israel. There is *continuity* and *wholeness* between Israel and the Church. Theologically, one cannot exist without the other in Christian thought. If an entity called "Old Israel" is no longer in God's favor, then God becomes a liar and can never be trusted again, for he promised Israel that she would be his people always. Though Israel be steeped in stubbornness and arrogance (as are *all* persons), God could not let his people go, as Hosea so graphically demonstrates in his acted out prophetic oracle with Gomer. God will not let Israel go now or later. The mainline churches need to hear this message as they develop relationships with their Jewish neighbors. The true Israel is a community of faith, rooted in the Torah, prophets, and writings. As communities of faith, the Church and Judaism are inseparably bound to one another, for they share a common history, a common experience, and a common God.

Part Three:
Where Can We
Go From Here?

"[May] the Lord Bless You and Keep You" Numbers 6:24

10

"He That is not Against You is For You" (Luke 9:50)

There has been animosity between Mormon Christians and Christians of other denominations since the inception of the Mormon church in 1830. Undoubtedly there were abuses and excesses on both sides. But as a member of the Reformed tradition, I feel the greater blame lies with persons who were not Mormon Christians. We of the Reformed tradition have no doctrines that claim superiority over our Christian brothers and sisters of any other denomination. We claim a particular and unique theological tradition that defines us as reformed and reforming Christians. But even so, God has not called us to stand in judgment over our neighbor, be that neighbor Christian or non-Christian. Rather God has called us to proclaim the good news of his presence with his people in Jesus Christ. To proclaim that message, we are not called to be negative or destructive. We are to be tools in the hands of the Spirit, as we share our faith and love with our brothers and sisters of whatever tradition and of whatever faith.

The Mormons, on the other hand, have a theological reason for feeling a certain sense of completeness and fullness in their tradition that other Christian traditions do not have. By now we understand that the restoration of the church, the return of the priesthood keys, the re-establishment of a living prophet on earth, are all seen by

Mormons as a restoration of the *eternal* priesthood and of the *eternal* plan of God upon the earth. Mormons truly believe that there is no salvation (meaning exaltation) outside the bounds of The Church of Jesus Christ of Latter-day Saints. Thus, in honesty to themselves, in obedience to their God, and out of love for their neighbor, both Christian and non-Christian, they can do naught else than proclaim the gospel of Jesus Christ and the restoration of his church as they know it and as they have experienced it. The true Church of Jesus Christ is defined by them as the Mormon church. All other churches, while they contain truth, do not contain the fullness of the truth. Therefore, they are fertile fields for evangelism, just as surely as is the non-Christian world.

Reformed Christians need not take offense at this. Our Mormon neighbors did not make up this doctrine. They believe it to have been given to them by God. We cannot ask them to be less than they are, and therefore we should learn to appreciate their theology and their beliefs, even if we cannot agree totally with all of them. There is no necessity for us to separate ourselves from our Mormon neighbors, for if we do we will only find ourselves exacerbating the condition of separation that began over 150 years ago with the founding of the Mormon church. Worse, we are repudiating our own claims to have Christian love. Instead, we should reach out in love and appreciation to our Mormon neighbors, and in doing so we will discover a response that is filled with love, compassion, and respect for us.

To encourage or practice separation from our Mormon Christian neighbors is also a denial of the Reformed confession of faith. The constitution of The Presbyterian Church (USA) states that the Church Universal is composed of persons who confess Jesus Christ as their Lord and Savior (Book of Order, G-4.0101). That is all it says. No questions of congruence with theological propositions and dogmatic statements are imposed. Just as the Christians of the early Church were Christian by virtue of their *confession* of Jesus as Lord, so also all persons who confess him as Lord in this day are Christian, regardless of their theological stances. To attempt to deny our Mormon neighbors the right to stand beside us as members of the Christian tradition, would be a denial of our own claim to be Christian. Finally, it is ironic that the Church has permitted all sorts of extreme theological positions to fall under the rubric of "Christian" (e.g., the "God is Dead" movement), and yet some persons still wish to deny that Mormons are Christian, when, in fact, virtually all their doctrines have some precedent in the history of the Church.

"Has Not God Made Foolish the Wisdom of the World?" *(I Corinthians 1:20)*

In recent months we who live in the American west and southwest have seen an ever increasing tide of anti-Mormon sentiment being expressed by some of our Christian brothers and sisters. The thesis is trumpeted that Mormons are not Christians because they do not believe the same things that these persons do, and that they do not believe in the "real Christ of the Bible." What is being said is that Mormons do not hold the same theological positions as do their opponents, and thus if they are not *theologically* "correct," they obviously cannot be Christian. But if one takes that stance, where does one stop? If one believes that Mormons are not Christians because they do not hold the same view of the Trinity that persons of the Catholic or Reformed traditions do, does that not also mean that the early believers in the first two or three centuries were not Christian, since the full trinitarian doctrine did not originate for several hundred years? If one claims that Mormons are not Christian, because they hold that there is subordinationism within the Godhead, and that the Father, Son, and Holy Ghost are not of one essence, does this also mean that members of the Eastern Orthodox tradition are non-Christian, because they do not hold our western theological position?

To make participation in the life of the Christian Church solely dependent upon "proper doctrine" and "proper knowl-

143

edge" is to be a gnostic. Gnostics believed that it was *right knowledge* which saved, and that if one had proper knowledge, then it mattered little what one actually did in one's life. There could be a radical separation between one's knowledge of God and one's activities in daily life. Paul spoke sharply against this position, stating that it was neither knowledge nor wisdom that unified people and God. Rather, it was in fact the folly of God and the foolishness of God, when viewed from a worldly perspective, that brought about this unity (I Cor. 1:17–31). True salvation is to live in a *relationship* with Jesus Christ, a relationship that Christ himself creates which is not dependent upon our actions or our beliefs. That relationship is created by Christ's Spirit, and it is the Holy Spirit who gives us a witness to Jesus Christ as the Son of God. That is the only knowledge we need to appropriate Christ's acts for us in his life, death, and resurrection. Indeed, anti-Mormon movements, anti-Catholic movements, anti-Jewish movements, or anti-Muslim movements, are all a denial of the power of the Holy Spirit, for when we move against other people in anger or bitterness or even in pious arrogance, we act as if we do not believe what our own religion affirms—i.e., that it is the Holy Spirit who converts and makes a people new. In our arrogance we hold ourselves up as the agents of conversion, rather than the servants of the Holy Spirit, and we become instruments of hate when Christ instead calls us to love and forgive.

"To [God] Be The Glory Forever" (Romans 11:36)

Ultimately, God and God alone controls this world, our destinies, and our faith. From this study we should be able to affirm that Jesus Christ is not limited by our theologies or our supposed knowledge. We all stand in relationship to the one Truth as long as we stand in relationship to Jesus Christ. Truth is not a series of propositional statements, but rather the person of Christ himself. To believe that God is bound to our limited understandings and to our limited structures, is to believe in a very limited God. We each, as Reformed and

Mormon Christians, can affirm the places and the structures wherein we have met our God and his Christ. But we cannot be sure that God does not meet, claim, and use people in other places and in other structures. Much in each of our traditions teaches and demonstrates otherwise. We can most assuredly affirm that God has used the Christians of the Mormon tradition and their structures to proclaim his gospel to the world, regardless of whether we can agree with all the propositional statements that are attendant to its theology. Similarly, we should be able to affirm that God has most assuredly worked through the Christians of the Reformed tradition to proclaim his gospel in all the world, once again whether we agree with all of its theological propositions or not. As much as we would like to, we cannot limit what God can do, for he is infinite, and we are finite.

The task of the Church's theological enterprise is always to seek in faith a deeper understanding of the object of our faith. We must constantly seek a deeper understanding of what God says to us as he confronts us in Jesus Christ. For that theological search to be effective, we must be able to sit down with our fellow Christians, of whatever denomination, and share the depths of the insights that we have gained from our individual walks with our Lord. If one believes that the Holy Spirit leads into all truth, then one need not fear such an interchange. One need not fear that personal faith will become polluted and contaminated by the faith of another person, for the Holy Spirit will blow away the chaff and keep the kernel. In quiet moments of theological sharing, we who are Reformed Christians and Mormon Christians may come to a deepened faith in our Lord Jesus Christ. It is highly probable that we each will be confirmed in our own traditions, for what our traditions really affirm is our *experience* with our God. That experience precedes and follows all analytic theology and all sophisticated understanding. Therefore, let us never stop talking with one another; let us never stop searching together for our common Lord, Jesus Christ.

There is no reason that Mormon Christians and Christians of other denominations cannot have open and productive relationships with one another, as long as they are willing to live under Christ's Lordship and by the guidance of his Spirit. In Christ, there is oneness with diversity. There is unity with variety. To accept our unity under the common Lordship of Jesus Christ does not require that we shed or do away with any of the things that are sacred to our individual traditions. All it requires is that we learn the lesson of I Cor. 13:4–7 (RSV) which says, "Love is patient and kind; it is not jealous or conceited or proud; love is not ill-mannered or selfish or irritable; love does not keep a record of wrongs; love is not happy with evil, but is happy with the truth. Love never gives up; and its faith, hope and patience never fail." In our common bond found in Jesus Christ, let us love one another.

Epilog

In this study we have seen that there are many similarities and many differences between Christians of the Mormon tradition and Christians of the Reformed tradition. The similarities are most clearly highlighted by the chart on page 102 which shows the major events of salvation history to be congruent. At the same time, the same chart shows many differences, particularly as we focus on the nature of God, the role of the fall, the extent of Christ's atonement, and the status of humanity before God in the afterlife. For all those differences, we must return to the reality that *theologies* do not make Christians, but rather *Jesus Christ* through his Holy Spirit makes Christians.

Thus, even though we differ in our Christian traditions on the theological issues, there are still many points where we can meet on beliefs, on issues, and on values. If we walk together in our common faith in Jesus Christ, we will find that we strengthen our communities, our churches, and our individual faiths. Rubbing shoulders with our religiously diverse neighbor does not diminish us. Rather it expands us, stretches us, and makes us better participants in Christ's Universal Church.

While there is commonality among us, there are also differences. We should be able to rejoice in those differences. In them lies the opportunity for us to lead one another to new horizons and to new insights, as we share in love the things that are most sacred to us. With the common belief that the Holy Spirit is the final authority in all issues of religious truth, we can relax while he bears his infallible witness to us through the pages of Holy Scripture, be we Christians of the Reformed tradition or Christians of the Mormon tradition.

In summary, it is hoped that this book may bring understanding to people of both the Mormon and Reformed traditions. If it has, it is my prayer that we will be able to extend the right hand of Christian fellowship to our neighbors of whatever faith, in the name of Jesus Christ, the Prince of Peace. In closing, we would do well to contemplate the words of two deeply committed servants of Jesus Christ —Joseph Smith and St. Francis of Assisi.

> We are always to be aware of those prejudices which sometimes so strangely present themselves and are so congenial to human nature against our friends, neighbors, and brethren of the world who choose to differ from us in opinion and in matters of faith. Our religion is between us and our God. Their religion is between them and their God. There is a love from God that should be exercised toward those of our faith who walk uprightly which is peculiar to itself but it is without prejudice. It also gives scope to the mind which enables us to conduct ourselves with greater liberality towards all that are not of our faith than what they exercise towards one another. These principles approximate closer to the mind of God because it is like God or Godlike (*Teachings*, p. 147).

> All I can offer the world is a good heart and a good hand. Mormons can testify whether I am willing to lay down my life for a Mormon. If it has been demonstrated that I have been willing to die for a Mormon, I am bold to declare before heaven that I am just as ready to die for a Presbyterian, a Baptist, or any other denomination. It is a love of liberty that inspires my soul . . . Wherein do you differ from others in your religious views? In reality and essence we do not differ so far in our religious views but that we could drink into one principle of love . . . If I esteem mankind to be in error, shall I bear them down? No. I will lift them up and each in his own way if I cannot persuade him my way is better! I will ask no man to believe as I do. Do you believe in Jesus Christ? So do I. Christians should cultivate the friendship with others and will do it (Andrew F. Ehat and Lyndon W. Cook, eds., *The Words of Joseph Smith*, [Provo: Religious Studies Center, 1980], p. 229, July 9, 1843).

Lord, make me an instrument of your peace.

> Where there is hatred—let me sow love.
> Where there is injury—pardon.
> Where there is doubt—faith.
> Where there is despair—hope.
> Where there is darkness—light.
> Where there is sadness—joy.

O Divine Master, grant that I may not so much seek

> To be consoled—as to console.
> To be understood—as to understand.
> To be loved—as to love.

For

> It is in giving—that we receive.
> It is in pardoning—that we are pardoned.
> It is in dying—that we are born to eternal life.

. . . St. Francis of Assisi

Bibliography

The following bibliography is not intended to be exhaustive in either the Reformed tradition or the Mormon tradition. Those books suggested in the Reformed tradition are ones that have meant a great deal to the author in his own spiritual growth and development. Most can be digested by a person seriously interested in Reformed theology. The list of Mormon works comes primarily from the bibliography in Reflections on Mormonism edited by Truman G. Madsen and published by the Religious Studies Center at Brigham Young University (1978).

Reformed Works

Baillie, D. M. *God Was in Christ*. 2nd rev. ed. New York: Charles Scribner's Sons, 1948.

Balthasar, Hans Urs von. *The Theology of Karl Barth*. Trans. John Drury. Garden City: Doubleday & Company, Inc. 1972.

Barth, Karl. *Church Dogmatics*. 13 vols. Edinburgh: T & T Clark. (For the advanced student).

_____. *Credo*. New York: Charles Scribner's Sons, 1962.

_____. *Dogmatics in Outline*. Trans. G. T. Thomson. New York: Harper & Row, Publishers, 1959.

_____. *The Humanity of God*. Richmond: John Knox Press, 1966.

_____. *The Knowledge of God and the Service of God*. Trans. J. L. M. Haire and Ian Henderson. London: Hodder and Stoughton Publishers, 1955.

_____. *Protestant Thought: From Rouseau to Ritschl*. Trans. Brian Cozens. New York: Simon and Schuster, 1969.

_____. *The Word of God and the Word of Man*. Trans. Douglas Horton. New York: Harper & Brothers, 1957.

Berdyaev, Nicolas. *The Destiny of Man*. Trans. Natalie Duddington. New York: Harper & Row, Publishers, 1960.

Brunner, Emil. *Dogmatics*. Trans. Olive Wyon. 3 vols. Philadelphia: The Westminster Press, n.d.

————. *Our Faith*. Trans. John W. Rilling. New York: Charles Scribner's Sons, n.d.

Calvin, John. *Institutes of the Christian Religion*. Trans. Ford Lewis Battles. 2 vols. Philadelphia: The Westminster Press, 1967.

Dillenberger, John. *Martin Luther. Selections from His Writings*. Garden City: Doubleday & Company, Inc., 1961.

Hartwell, Herbert. *The Theology of Karl Barth: An Introduction*. Philadelphia: The Westminster Press, 1962.

Luther, Martin. *Lectures on Romans*. Ed. and trans. Wilhelm Pauck. Philadelphia: The Westminster Press, 1961.

Niebuhr, Reinhold. *The Nature and Destiny of Man*. 2 vols. New York: Charles Scribner's Sons, 1964.

Mormon Works

Theology and Interpretation

Bennion, Lowell L. *The Religion of the Latter-day Saints*. 2d ed. Salt Lake City: LDS Department of Education, 1964.

Ludlow, Daniel H., ed. *Latter-day Prophets Speak*. Salt Lake City: Bookcraft, 1951.

Madsen, Truman G. *Eternal Man*. Salt Lake City: Deseret Book, 1970.

————. "The Meaning of Christ—The Truth, the Way, the Life: An Analysis of B. H. Roberts' Unpublished Masterwork." Reprinted from *BYU Studies*, 15 (Spring 1975).

McConkie, Bruce R. *Mormon Doctrine*. 2d ed. Salt Lake City: Bookcraft, 1966.

McMurrin, Sterling M. *The Philosophical Foundations of Mormon Theology*. Salt Lake City: University of Utah Press, 1959.

————. *The Theological Foundations of the Mormon Religion*. Salt Lake City: University of Utah Press, 1965.

Nibley, Hugh W. "Baptism for the Dead in Ancient Times." *Improvement Era* 51 (December 1948): 786 ff.; 52 (January 1949): 24 ff.; (February 1949): 90 ff.: (March 1949): 146 ff.; (April 1949): 212 ff.

————. "The Passing of the Church: Forty Variations on an Unpopular Theme." *Church History* 30 (June 1961): 1–24.

————. *The World and the Prophets*. Salt Lake City: Deseret Book, 1962.

_____. *Nibley on the Timely and the Timeless.* Brigham Young University Religious Studies Center Monograph Series, vol. 1. Provo, Utah: Brigham Young University Religious Studies Center, 1978.

Palmer, Spencer J., ed. *Deity and Death.* Brigham Young University Religious Studies Center Monograph Series, vol. 2. Provo, Utah: Brigham Young University Religious Studies Center, 1978.

Pratt, Parley P. *Key to the Science of Theology.* 9th ed. Salt Lake City: Deseret Book, 1965.

Roberts, Brigham H. *The Atonement.* The Seventy's Course in Theology, vol. 4. Salt Lake City: Deseret News Press, 1911.

_____. *Divine Immanence and the Holy Ghost.* The Seventy's Course in Theology, vol. 5. Salt Lake City: Deseret News Press, 1912.

_____. *The Doctrine of Deity.* The Seventy's Course in Theology, vol. 3. Salt Lake City: Caxton Press, 1910.

Smith, Joseph. *Teachings of the Prophet Joseph Smith.* Compiled by Joseph Fielding Smith. Salt Lake City: Deseret Book, 1961.

Smith, Joseph F. *Gospel Doctrine: Selections from the Sermons and Writings of Joseph F. Smith.* Salt Lake City: Deseret Book, 1939.

Smith, Joseph Fielding. *Answers to Gospel Questions.* 5 vols. Salt Lake City: Deseret Book, 1957–1966.

_____. *Doctrines of Salvation,* compiled by Bruce R. McConkie. 3 vols. Salt Lake City: Bookcraft, 1954–1965.

Talmage, James Edward. *The Great Apostasy Considered in the Light of Scriptural and Secular History.* Salt Lake City: Deseret News Press, 1968.

_____. *The Philosophical Basis of "Mormonism"; an Address Delivered by Invitation Before the Congress of Religious Philosophies, Held in Connection with the Panama-Pacific International Exposition, San Francisco, California, July 29, 1915.*

_____. *A Study of the Articles of Faith, Being a Consideration of the Principal Doctrines of The Church of Jesus Christ of Latter-day Saints.* Salt Lake City: The Church of Jesus Christ of Latter-day Saints, 1960.

Tullis, F. LaMond, ed. *Mormonism: A Faith for All Cultures.* Provo, Utah: Brigham Young University Press, 1978.

Widtsoe, John A. *Evidences and Reconciliations.* Compiled by G. Homer Durham. Salt Lake City: Bookcraft, 1960.

_____. *A Rational Theology, as Taught by The Church of Jesus Christ of Latter-day Saints.* Salt Lake City: Deseret Book, 1965.

Young, Brigham. *Discourses of Brigham Young.* Compiled by John A. Widtsoe. Salt Lake City: Deseret Book, 1961.

History

Allen, James B., and Leonard, Glen N., eds. *The Story of the Latter-day Saints.* Salt Lake City: Deseret Book, 1976.

Allen, James B., and Hill, Marvin A., eds. *Mormonism and American Culture.* New York: Harper and Row, 1972.

Anderson, Nels. *Desert Saints: The Mormon Frontier in Utah.* Chicago: University of Chicago Press, 1942.

Anderson, Richard Lloyd. *Joseph Smith's New England Heritage.* Salt Lake City: Deseret Book, 1971.

Arrington, Leonard J.; Fox, Feramorz Y.; and May, Dean L. *Building the City of God: Community and Cooperation Among the Mormons.* Salt Lake City: Deseret Book, 1976.

Arrington, Leonard J. *Great Basin Kingdom: An Economic History of the Latter-day Saints, 1830–1900.* Cambridge, Mass.: Harvard University Press, 1958.

Arrington, Leonard J. and Bitton, Davis. *The Mormon Experience: A History of the Latter-day Saints.* New York: Alfred A. Knopf, 1970.

Backman, Milton V., Jr. *American Religions and the Rise of Mormonism.* Salt Lake City: Deseret Book, 1965.

Barrett, Ivan J. *Joseph Smith and the Restoration: A History of the Church to 1846.* 2d ed. Provo, Utah: Brigham Young University Press, 1973.

Berrett, William E. *The Restored Church.* Salt Lake City: Deseret Book, 1969.

Cross, Whitney. *The Burned-Over District: The Social and Intellectual History of Enthusiastic Religion in Western New York, 1800–1850.* New York: Harper and Row, 1950.

Hill, Donna. *Joseph Smith: The First Mormon.* New York: Doubleday, 1977.

Jenson, Andrew. *Encyclopedic History of The Church of Jesus Christ of Latter-day Saints.* Salt Lake City: Deseret Book, 1941.

Larson, Gustive O. *The Americanization of Utah.* San Marino, California: Huntington Library, 1971.

Mulder, William, and Mortensen, A. Russell, eds. *Among the Mormons: Historic Accounts by Contemporary Observers.* New York: Alfred A. Knopf, 1958.

McKiernan, F. Mark; Blair, Alma R.; and Edwards, Paul M., eds. *The Restoration Movement: Essays in Mormon History.* Lawrence, Kansas: Coronado Press, 1973.

Paul, Rodman. "The Mormons as a Theme in Western Historical Writings." *The Journal of American History* 54 (December 1967): 511–23.

Roberts, B. H. *A Comprehensive History of the Church.* 6 vols. Salt Lake City: Deseret News Press, 1930.

Smith, Joseph. *History of The Church of Jesus Christ of Latter-day Saints.* Edited with an introduction and notes by B. H. Roberts. 7 vols. Salt Lake City: Deseret Book, 1902–1932.

Taylor, P. A. M. *Expectations Westward: The Mormons and the Emigration of Their British Converts in the 19th Century.* Edinburgh and London: Oliver and Boyd, 1965.

West, Ray B., Jr. *Kingdom of the Saints: The Story of Brigham Young and the Mormons.* New York: Viking Press, 1957.